COMPOSITION AND RESISTANCE

composition & resistance

EDITED BY

C. Mark Hurlbert

AND

Michael Blitz

BOYNTON/COOK PUBLISHERS

HEINEMANN

Portsmouth, NH

Boynton/Cook Publishers, Inc.
A Subsidiary of
Heinemann Educational Books, Inc.
361 Hanover Street, Portsmouth, NH 03801-3959
Offices and agents throughout the world

Library of Congress Cataloging-in-Publication Data
Composition and resistance/edited by C. Mark Hurlbert and Michael Blitz.
    p.   cm.
    Includes bibliographical references.
    ISBN 0-86709-281-5
    1. English language — Rhetoric — Study and teaching.   2. Rhetoric — Political
aspects.   3. Rhetoric — Social aspects.   I. Hurlbert, C. Mark.   II. Blitz, Michael.
PE1404.C623   1991
808'.042'07 — dc20   91-19114
                                                                                CIP

Printed in the United States of America.
91   92   93   94   95   9   8   7   6   5   4   3   2   1

To Terry and Roland and Karen and Daina

Contents

Foreword

Judith Fetterley

I was asked to write the foreword to this book because I am the author of *The Resisting Reader*. As a resisting reader, I might be presumed to have some interest in the connections between resistance and composition. Which I do. I start with a reflection and a question about my own writing practice. When I finished *The Resisting Reader* I thought long and hard about the politics involved in continuing to occupy the stance of a resisting reader, which as I had defined it meant continuing to write about the canonical tradition in nineteenth- and twentieth-century American literature, a tradition white, male, middle-class. I finally decided not to continue to work on this tradition but rather to explore the texts written by American women during the nineteenth century. My second book, *Provisions*, collected texts written by American women between 1830 and 1865 and paired the texts with lengthy interpretative essays. I ended my introduction to *Provisions* with "A Personal Note on Process" in which I described my difficulties in developing a voice for writing the book. I did not wish to be a resisting reader in relation to this tradition. Goddess knows there was enough of that in the comments of the various critics, mostly male, who had over the years ignored or trivialized the work of nineteenth-century American women writers. Instead I wished to write about these texts in such a way as to persuade others of their interest and value. To do this I had to develop an image of the reader as lover and to learn to write appreciations rather than critiques. Or, to put it in the language I used in my note, I had to learn to write as a "woman," not as a "man."

I am not nearly as well known for my work on the texts of nineteenth-century American women as I am for my work on the texts written by American men. There could be and probably are many reasons for this. But here I would like to explore briefly just one possible reason. Perhaps it is the case that resistance, at least of the kind I practiced in *The Resisting Reader*, serves an essentially conservative purpose. The stance of the antagonist is classically male; the voice of the critic, rational, angry, ironic, in sufficient command of the material so as to critique it, is essentially male; and the act of resistance finally serves to foreground and reassert the very material being resisted. As evidence take the comment of a male colleague who finally read

The Resisting Reader and said, "Wow, this is great; it gives me a new way to teach Hemingway!" Who wants to hear the wimpy voice of appreciation? At a recent conference I heard a brilliant woman explain her love of resistance by invoking the metaphor of brook and dam. Dam the brook and you get a lake and the possibility of hydroelectric power. But I wanted to resist her love of resistance by murmuring that brooks are nice too.

Yet I have come to realize that my "natural," or "default," mode as a writer is the voice and style I developed in *The Resisting Reader*. If I don't think through the issues behind the voice I choose to respond to any given text in any given situation, I will respond as a resisting reader. In a recent conversation on the teaching of writing, a colleague proposed that instead of trying to teach students the appropriate voice and style for a given assignment we seek rather to discover the student's natural writing voice and then suggest assignments appropriate for that voice. A bold proposal, but of interest to me primarily as a way of focusing my thoughts on the issue of "natural" writing voice. In writing *Provisions* was I engaged in a complex act of self-resistance based on my assessment of what currently constitutes the most politically valuable mode for feminist criticism? Is it useful to teach our students how to resist their "natural" voice? Is it finally wise for me to so resist my "natural" voice, or am I in effect disempowering myself?

Interestingly enough, I am not particularly interested in resistance as a mode of talk. As a teacher I like to pose genuinely open-ended questions and to generate genuinely open-ended conversation among myself and the students in my class. The language I invoke to describe what I try to accomplish in the classroom includes such phrases as "a community of learners" engaged in "problem posing" to explore areas of mutual interest in an atmosphere of "openness" and "play." For, indeed, certain kinds of fun are only possible when everyone is willing to play the believing game, and I do like to have fun. I see this issue quite clearly in my family situation. I have one child who frequently approaches the family project from the stance of a resister, whose first response to any proposal is often "no, I don't want to do that, it is boring and stupid." And I have one child who usually agrees to play the family game. While I respect the stance of the resisting child and recognize it as her way of maintaining identity and individuality, her response severely constricts what we can do. Moreover, in response to her response I tend to get hooked into a negative cycle of whining at her for whining at me or of ceasing altogether to propose any projects. Having taught a course on "mothering and reading and writing and teaching," I am sensitive to the similarities between the family scene and the classroom scene. I do better with the child who doesn't resist and I do better with the class that agrees to strive to become a community of learners. But then there often comes that point in the happy classroom when a student whom I respect, whom I know to be serious and playful and seriously playful and playfully serious, objects with anger to something I have said, and I have to reassess my entire project because I have to wonder how much resistance I have silenced by my desire/demand for a community of believers. And I have to ask whether such silencing does not in fact undermine the very goals I had in creating the non-resisting classroom in the first place.

In writing this I have come to realize something exceedingly obvious. I "naturally" adopt the stance of resistance when I am in the role of student, and I "naturally" adopt the stance of non-resistance when I am in the role of teacher. If role determines stance, how can teachers ever genuinely teach students to resist and how can students ever genuinely cooperate with teachers? As a feminist teacher teaching women students to deconstruct and resist sexism, I can sometimes find an answer to this question. For a radical feminist, daily life offers endless occasions for resistance, and thus I can genuinely occupy the position of student in relation to such occasions. But what happens to the concept of resistance and to the possibility of teacher as student when a male student invokes the model of feminism as resistance to resist feminism and the feminist teacher?

I recently had the experience of teaching a course designed in part to introduce students to the ways in which racism and sexism structure academic institutions. The majority of the students in the class were women, but the loudest voices, even when they were silent, were those of some men in the class, not all, whose agenda eventually took over. Unfortunately, the very model I proposed of the class as a community of learners worked against the goals I had in making such a proposal, for the male students were able to present their complaints as consonant with the genre of problem posing and to present themselves as sharing and representing the interests of the larger community. They positioned themselves, not as men concerned with the implication of the issues we were discussing for their own current and anticipated privilege, but rather as sensitive fellow feminists resisting the agenda of a power-hungry professor. Since women have been so thoroughly conditioned to place the interests of men before their own, indeed to find it quite difficult to distinguish their own interests from those of men as individuals or collectively, invoking students and teacher as the operative oppositional categories to replace those of women and men proved simple and effective. Most women in the class found it comfortable to identify with the apparently gender-neutral category of "student" and to join in the opposition to the category of "teacher." Moreover, since women are additionally socialized to respond with comfort to men any time they cry out that they have been hurt, it was equally simple for the men to get most women in the class to support them in their claim that they had been marginalized.

In this context, resistance had the effect of simply reinscribing the sexism I was trying to deconstruct. The women in the class were effectively silenced from voicing any of the concerns they might have had as women in relation to men as colleagues. And they were effectively engaged in a process of identifying with men and against themselves, for many women in the class were planning careers as teachers. Ironically, of course, the class evolved as it did precisely because the men understood and took full advantage of their power as men. Male students can count not only on sympathy from women students but on support from male authorities when they charge women teachers with reverse discrimination in the college classroom. And they can count on the fear that frequently leads women to self-destruct rather than to risk offending men to effectively suppress any challenge to their behavior.

So I can't make a fetish of resistance. I admire the work Mark and Michael have done in putting this book together, and I admire the book's design. And I am sympathetic to the political agenda I sense behind the book's existence and design. Reading *Composition and Resistance* has inspired me to think harder about my practice as a teacher of writing and to feel more comfortable with my own process as a writer. I appreciate the opportunity it has given me to compose a meditation on the subject of composition and resistance. I suspect that is at least one of the ways Mark and Michael would wish the book to be read.

Acknowledgments

Thanks to Peter Stillman and Bob Boynton for their support and encouragement; to Nancy Sheridan for her hard work; to Geneva Smitherman for advice and inspiration; to Janice O'Donnell from Winthrop Hospital, Mineola, New York, and Marge Byrd, Mercy College, Albany, New York, for the use of the transcription machines; to Kim Ginther-Webster from the Engineering and Science Library at Carnegie Mellon University, Bill Webster from WMXP, 100.7 Pittsburgh, Pennsylvania (Mix Jamz!), Dan Lowe from Allegheny Community College, Pittsburgh, and Jane McCafferty from the University of Pittsburgh for their assistance in editing transcripts; to Agnes Malicka and Alan Luckey, Indiana University of Pennsylvania, for their help in typing the prospectus and transcribing the Seattle roundtable; to everyone in the Office of the Graduate School and Research at IUP for funding some of the photocopying; to the Holiday Inn, Crowne Plaza, in Seattle, the Best Western Hallmark Hotel in Baltimore, and the Palmer House in Chicago for the meeting rooms; to Direct Plumbing Corporation, Hicksville, New York, for the use of photocopying equipment at critical times; to the IUP and John Jay College English Departments for photocopying and mailing assistance; to Lil Brannon, Karyn Hollis, and Louise Wetherbee Phelps for their suggestions; and most of all to the participants who contributed their writings and committed themselves to participating in the dialogues at the CCCC convention in Seattle, 1989, the NCTE Annual Convention in Baltimore, 1989, and the CCCC convention in Chicago, 1990.

Editors' Notes

Read the transcripts as drama featuring:

James A. Berlin, Purdue University
Michael Blitz, John Jay College of Criminal Justice,
  City University of New York
Miriam T. Chaplin, Rutgers University, Camden
Jeff Golub, Shorecrest High School, Seattle, Washington
Joseph Harris, University of Pittsburgh
C. Mark Hurlbert, Indiana University of Pennsylvania
C. H. Knoblauch, State University of New York at Albany
Nancy Mack, Wright State University
Cecilia Rodríguez Milanés, Indiana University of Pennsylvania
Stephen M. North, State University of New York at Albany
Louann Reid, Douglas County High School, Colorado
Donna Singleton, Southern Illinois University at Edwardsville
James Sledd, University of Texas, Austin
Kurt Spellmeyer, Rutgers University, New Brunswick
J. Elspeth Stuckey, Clemson University and South Carolina State
  College South Carolina Cross-Age Tutoring Project
Marian Yee, Ann Arbor, Rutgers University, New Brunswick
James Thomas Zebroski, Syracuse University

Thanks to Sue Ellen Holbrook for permission to publish part of her abstract in James Sledd's "How We Apples Swim."

1

Resisting Composure

C. Mark Hurlbert
Michael Blitz

We pose this book as a set of what Joan Cocks calls "points of aggravation" (65). The book poses problems about its composition, and the compositions we have included in it raise questions about maintaining composure in a troubling profession. In spite of the fact that writers experience all sorts of turmoil, uncertainty, and discomfort when they—we—write, writing instruction, particularly in textbooks, attempts to make composing less aggravating and more programmatic, merely a matter of acquiring useful, marketable skills. This kind of instruction serves mainly to industrialize composing by teaching students to assemble meaning, whether linearly or recursively, rather than to challenge the politics and economics of the markets in which these skills are supposed to be useful.

When we, Mark and Michael, discuss what we are doing when we write, we talk about composing as the way in which we attempt to introduce incoherence—a loss of composure—into "the entrenched order of things" (Cocks 66). As Joan Cocks notes, the kinds of ideas most likely to offer "openings of resistance" are those that prove to be "too elusive...too shapeless...to be sanctified" (66). With this in mind, we have attempted a book in which, rather than making a settlement within the field of composition, we resist ending events and settling differences. As editors and contributors, the two of us have had to resist our impulses to close the book. Even as we are now revising this beginning, we are talking one another out of trying to tie all the loose ends together. And there *are* loose ends. The writers and speakers in this book start things we can't claim to have finished.

Susan Stewart's observations about collections, in her book *On Longing*, suggested to us a useful way to think about the book we were planning. Observing that any collection is "a form involving the re-framing of objects within a world of attention and manipulation of context," she distinguishes between the "autonomous" collection, conceived to establish "a dialectic of inside and outside," and the "open-ended" collection, which "tends toward infinity or series" (151–155), one to which collectors invite even *long for*, new additions, a collection which, gradually, becomes less distinct from things "outside" it. From the beginning of *Composition and Resistance*, our aim has been to collect a set of events. Participants would meet for a series of three roundtables, which the two of us would tape, transcribe, and edit for inclusion in this book. In addition, participants would contribute a fairly brief chapter that they could revise after each roundtable. The two of us wondered what kind of work composition teachers would do together if we read each other's drafts, questioned one another's rhetoric and politics, challenged the difference(s) between what we were writing and what we were discussing at the roundtables, and made the same kinds of demands for revision that we generally make of our students.

As editors, the two of us were, in a sense, anticipating that this collection would fall apart, that in important ways it would fail to present a coherent discipline, a unified field, or a specific set of useful practices. This is the value. Composition can be something other than the discipline in which our students practice or simulate a form of production they may need later. Composition is, as all compositions are, a set of practices that are part of the rhetoric of the institution, influenced and informed by — and enacted in resistance to — other practices in which ideologies are played out and contested.

Composition and Resistance developed out of the participants' genuine longing to do *social* work. It grew out of our exasperation with social problems we think teaching could do something about and out of desire to find and to make and to support solidarities among those with whom we live and work. As a number of participants observed in various terms, we can attempt such solidarities only in resistance to the ways that institutions of higher education effectively transform individuals' work into profiles of performance among "the students," "the faculty," and "the staff." We wanted — and need — to look for ways to talk, to teach, to listen, and to write that do not suppress the voices of others. The book has grown into a kind of script, a record of working out loud which, as the two of us read and edit it, seems to invite a performative reading in response. It is a chaotic, noisy, and *troubled* book. And for the record, now that the two of us have seen the parts become the book, we argue that a lot of us are going to have to be a lot noisier and make a lot bigger commotion if we hope to resist powers that can so easily restore us to order.

James Sledd said it in Seattle:

> I suggest that another thing we have to resist is ourselves.... We build into ourselves, like it or not, the very structures that we hope to attack. The other thing I think we have to resist is the system that builds itself into us.

The "chapters" and the conversations in this book sound and look peculiar together. In our thinking, this strangeness suggests a useful poetics of composition where the composition is read as a record of public and private action and counter-action. It is the site in which people struggle against what Kenneth Burke refers to as the "recalcitrance" of the very materials with which we compose (255). We can recontextualize Burke's notion of recalcitrance in the local work of teaching composition: students write with the strategy to *overcome* what they perceive is the teacher's — the institution's — *recalcitrance* to accept and to participate *in* the events of their writing. Composition teachers must continually find and make new ways to act in relation to the events, choices, and struggles to which any composition testifies. To begin, we must resist silent acquiescence — submission — to "standardization," to convenient ignorance of cultural diversity. "The United States has welded together diverse people and races, with their many tongues and cultures — including even the 35 million African descendants of an enslaved population, including even the millions of descendants of Native American and Spanish intermixture," Geneva Smitherman reminds us. For too long educators have "mis—educated" students by failing to teach "what we *is* instead of what we *ain*" (119).

One of our students, Jerri, wrote a research paper by first listing fifteen passages quoted from books and articles dealing with her topic, on-the-job-training. She then devoted the rest of the paper to a series of very short paragraphs, each of which commented, often in very personal ways ("Studs [Terkel] should have talked to hookers in *my* neighborhood before he wrote this."), on one of the quotes. She concluded with a suggested reading list of texts that would, she said, talk about the topic better than she could. Jerri's paper does not argue by assembling a report on research, a paper arranged to support "pros" in order to defeat a "con." Instead, Jerri gathers a personal collection of moments of her reading of various texts and then points to the likelihood that her readers will need to move to still other texts. Her composition remains open at its "conclusion."

It would be easy — and probably customary — to argue that Jerri's research paper is improperly or incorrectly formed. Written responses to her paper ought to tell her how she should have constructed an effective argument proving a thesis, or at least how she should have organized her essay like the source material she had read. But Jerri's paper *challenges* us to wonder whether her writing wasn't somehow more intellectually useful and necessary to her than anything we might have required her to do. We would also argue that Jerri probably did understand those "unfulfilled" requirements. She defers, at the end of her paper, to the "real" authorities she knows she "should have" sounded like.

Jerri was both wildly courageous and, as the paper's ending suggests, suspicious of her own actions and choices. Jerri undercuts what she has done, but perhaps she does so because she anticipates that her readers — especially the teacher — will see through her inadequate mastery of the research paper. And no doubt Jerri has often had her worst misgivings about her abilities as a writer supported by her teachers' remarks. But Jerri's anti-conclusion points to another and perhaps more difficult problem. The strangeness of her paper's form requires serious, creative work from her readers, effort that composition teachers too often are discouraged from, unwilling to, or incapable of giving. There are still many people teaching composition who are inadequately trained to do it or too overloaded and powerless to do it well. The result is that unusual writings, such as Jerri's, never have the opportunity to alter the shape of our classrooms, schools, and society. Ron Silliman notes, "by difficulty, a writer makes it harder to be absorbed and commoditized" (Friedlander 40). The "good" composition is traditionally and precisely the one that *can* easily be "absorbed and commoditized." As one colleague said about Jerri's research paper, "Writers like this don't understand how *tedious* it is to *read* their papers." Colleagues such as this one, we argue, don't understand how unbearable they make our lives and the lives of our students. The result is that even more than a teacher's restrictive expectations, but also because of them, Jerri limits her abilities, her willingness, even her recognition of the need to make learning a personal act toward taking greater control of her life. And in an age in which the state and its big business partners regulate more and more of what is permissible to say and do, in what sense is teaching composition liberatory if students and teachers have already absorbed codes of silence?

Patrocinio Schweickart says that writing is an "arena of political struggle, a crucial component of the project of reinterpreting the world in order to change it" (39). Writing, itself, is a struggle in and *with* social order. It is a struggle to be heard, to make people pay attention, and to discover ways to attend to the domain of the possible. Teachers of writing must work with students to perceive these possibilities because these are, perhaps, our only hope for change. Through this work, students and teachers can challenge the expectations that cause any of us, as they did Jerri, to doubt our power and our abilities to use that power. "We can do," as poet Don Byrd suggests, "precisely what we have disciplined ourselves against — generating freshness in the world."

"Education is an act of love, and thus an act of courage," Paulo Freire tells us (38). Teachers do indeed need courage to make their classrooms safe places for students to use their power to speak out, to make noise, and to interpret it. They need courage to support the efforts of students as they try to turn their critical attention to social and political arenas. We all know administrators and colleagues who devote their careers to muffling noise, who see speaking and thinking "out of turn" as transgressions. (We both serve on college and departmental committees, supposedly devoted to the interests of students and/or vital educational issues, in which committee members spend far more time elaborately following Robert's rules of order than they do on making decisions and plans for change. It is both ironic and frustrating that making and seconding, calling the question, voting on and summarizing a *motion* can virtually *stall* the proceedings. Of course, as one of our own former teachers has said, "college committees are *supposed* to prevent good things from really happening.") We would counter by suggesting that such suppression betrays a fundamental cowardice. The two of us tell our students that remarks, even just the *sounds* people make — groans, laughter, "mmmhmms," which they might feel are stupid or are interruptions in the lesson plan — will work to make someone else think and say something meaningful in response. And we point out that getting dialogue started is a difficult and valuable — perhaps a loving — thing for anyone to do.

During the first hour of the Baltimore roundtable, participants frequently spoke the arguments they have lived with for a while and which did not, strictly speaking, invite dialogue so much as prompt a series of polite anecdotes. Clearly we were all uncomfortable. To observers we would have appeared to be playing the role of experts — cool, calm, and collected — that professionals typically take at conferences and in publications.

Knoblauch: Well, I mean there is — a lot of this can be talk.

Mack: Mmmhmm.

Knoblauch: — a lot of this can be safe, a lot of this can be — radical chic, face it. This is not harder to play than some other kind of school game —

Berlin: Oh, it is harder, I don't —

Knoblauch: Oh, maybe it's a *little* harder.

Berlin: It's a little harder, right? Yeah. [laughter]

North: He said from a hotel in Baltimore! He said in a hotel in Baltim —

Berlin: Oh, come on! Listen, this is costing me a lot of money. I mean I came here because I'm getting—the only reason I'm here is because this is an alternative. This is not the usual kind of conference format. I mean, it is costing me, *"he said"* [laughter] a hell of a lot of money to be here and *he better* get his money's worth. [laughter]

Knoblauch: We might have to hold ourselves to a much sterner standard than other people around this table. I mean, a white male academic with tenure has got to do a lot of fast talking to persuade himself that what he's doing constitutes some kind of serious social action with risks involved.

Berlin: Oh, well, listen, of course—

Knoblauch: An important thing—

Berlin: I mean, but we're talking about teaching now, or as teachers, right? We're starting where we are, right?

Finding a place to start did not ensure that we would have a place to go.

Stuckey: It's teachers of writing who can probably do more than teachers of anything else. Now the question is "why?" My answer is that it's not because writing is somehow human, or that it makes you somehow moral or gives you a transcendent take on the world. It's that the ways in which the major economies in the world exist now rest on writing, and—I hate this because I used to disagree with it—it's a matter of being able to use reading and writing as coercive and violent practices.

Spellmeyer: Well, if we're talking about people who maybe fund the university, or who—you know, Jim [Sledd] was talking about, earlier, these guys who are in a room and they hire the the, they hire the chancellor and the chancellor hires somebody else. I mean, knowledge doesn't belong to anybody, right?

Stuckey: Oh no, it certainly does!

Spellmeyer: Well, I don't think so. See I don't really believe that. I think that knowledge is up for grabs, and I think anybody can get it and use it, in a—I love this idea, you know, Foucault has this idea of what he calls the "tactical polyvalence of discourses." Knowledge that can be used in one context can be taken out of this context and used by very different groups. You see feminists doing this all the time, where they'll appropriate language of one group and use it in the service of something else. There's no reason you can't use the teaching of writing very differently.

Stuckey: But I certainly don't think that knowledge is free and available to the world.

Spellmeyer: I didn't say that. I said that it's open to many uses. In other words—

Stuckey: But who gets to use it? I mean that's a very important question. Who the hell gets to use it?

Elspeth Stuckey's statement that writing teachers are in a better position to act raises the question: what do we, as writing teachers, act upon? Did Elspeth mean to suggest that teaching students to write means arming them "to use reading and writing as coercive and violent practices"? Shouldn't we prepare our students to *resist* coercion and violence? How would we do that? If knowledge is up for grabs yet not really within everyone's reach, how can teachers prepare students to resist those uses of knowledge, by those who *can* "grab" it, which oppress others? How can we step outside what Joan Cocks calls the "regime of truth" that we inhabit, institutionalized perceptions, our "official consciousness" (64)?

James Sledd wrote to the two of us that educators should resist "familiar abuses" such as the exploitation of part-timers. However, the abuse of part-timers, of women, even of students in most universities is not only "familiar," but so much a part of the everyday business of the institution, that it may seem to be natural, which is to say invisible. Educators must make familiar abuses appear in all of their unnaturalness and ill-naturedness. We must be what Neil Postman and Charles Weingartner would call "crap detectors." As they put it, "an insensitivity to the unconscious effects of our 'natural' metaphors condemns us to highly constricted perceptions of how things are and, therefore, to highly limited alternative modes of behavior" (5). Such an "insensitivity" condemns others, too. If we can do anything as writing teachers and as writers, it should be to stop teaching students to underwrite the university, to stop demanding written material which can be easily *gathered* and *assessed*. We can teach writing as an event in which knowledge and form is preserved or resisted and changed. We can teach writing as the material out of which we not only (re)create ourselves and others, our understanding of culture, ethnicity, gender, sexuality, class, but also as the material with which we can resist these narratives when they do *not* accurately reflect our real lives.

North: I got a problem because I want to know what the opposite, then, of resistance is. You [Chaplin] say you resisted in order to become what you wanted to be. I understand that. But where do the images for who you'd like to be come from? And do you accept those? So the opposite of "resistance" is "acceptance"? Or not? That's what I want to know—

Chaplin: Yeah, I think it almost is acceptance because resistance requires a lot of strength, and I think that you get that strength from within yourself, but you also get it from the world view that you create as being part of other people who have also resisted, you see? So it's something that's almost inborn, but everybody doesn't have it, and I have many, many students who would rather accept than resist, so—

North: But you must have accepted something.

Chaplin: Of course I have.

North: But, I want to know if that's a negative thing.

Berlin: But see, the thing is, you're making a binary opposition with acceptance.

Mack: Right.

Berlin: It could be compliance.

Singleton: Acquiescence.

Berlin: Acquiescence, right.

Mack: Yeah.

Rodríguez Milanés: Right.

North: So, there are two choices in life, you can either —

Mack and Berlin: NO! NO! NO! [laughter]

Zebroski: I want to save "resistance" for some very specific uses. I don't want to use it when I talk about students not wanting to do something or myself not wanting to do something. I don't want to use it when I am talking about local conditions. I want to use it when I'm talking about social structures and their effect all across discourse. And I want to use that specifically in terms of, well, reigning social structures, ruling social structures, um, you know there are other things, but I think for me it gets down to talking and writing and dealing with issues like class, race, gender, sexualities. Issues where there's a privileged position that seems to be widely — not just accepted, but imposed on people who would prefer, perhaps, some other ways of living.

Sledd: Because I am aware of World War II, ["resistance"] has a very positive value — it's just splendid — and the gradual deterioration of the status of this term is an index of what's happened to our society.

Works Cited

Burke, Kenneth. *Permanence and Change: An Anatomy of Purpose*. 3rd ed. Berkeley: U of Cal P, 1984.

Byrd, Don. *The Poetics of Common Knowledge*. Unpublished manuscript.

Cocks, Joan. *The Oppositional Imagination: Feminism, Critique and Political Theory*. New York: Routledge, 1989.

Freire, Paulo. *Education for Critical Consciousness*. New York: Continuum, 1987.

Friedlander, Ben. "Laura Riding/Some Difficulties." *Women & Language*. Ed. Lyn Hejinian and Barret Watten. Spec. issue of *Poetics Journal* (4 May 1984): 35–42.

Postman, Neil, and Charles Weingartner. *Teaching as a Subversive Activity*. New York: Dell, 1969.

Schweickart, Patrocinio. "Reading Ourselves: Toward a Feminist Theory of Reading." *Gender and Reading: Essays on Readers, Texts, and Contexts*. Ed. Elizabeth A. Flynn and Patrocinio Schweickart. Baltimore: Johns Hopkins UP, 1986. 31–62.

Smitherman, Geneva. "The 'Mis-education of the Negro' — and You Too." *Not Only English: Affirming America's Multilingual Heritage*. Ed. Harvey A. Daniels. Urbana: NCTE, 1990. 109–120.

Stewart, Susan. *On Longing: Narratives of the Miniature, the Gigantic, the Souvenir, the Collection*. Baltimore: Johns Hopkins UP, 1984.

Knoblauch: Well, you know "resistance" may characterize in one way or another our relationship with some social reality, but I wonder what words characterize our implicating of our students in our resistances. You know, they're not resisting, except maybe us. I wonder, I mean, when we speak of resistance—the odd thing about our use of that word in this kind of context when we're all classroom teachers, is that what we're doing is, has, an odd and an indirect relationship to our students. And I wonder what words we can use to characterize that relationship. They get to go along with our resistance.

Mack: Yeah, I think I know what you're talking about. I got in a dialogue with someone else about this and it really concerned me. It seems like this is something that university people have "discovered." And so we'll have "remedial resistance" [laughter] [for] our students who don't know how to do this. And I really have problems with that, because of course it gives us the position of privilege. I really feel that students do resist, and I think that's one of the things that's so interesting. Education goes two ways in the classroom. And that's why I think I want to know more about how they resist and how they view their resistance. I mean it's really wrong to assume that only well-educated university people see through the power relations in society. My students see these same things but they react in different ways: they rationalize things, they get drunk, they do subversive activities in the classroom like giving the teacher the finger subtly in... you know what I'm saying. They have ways of resisting, but we may not acknowledge those as legitimate ways.

Knoblauch: We use the same ones, don't we, more or less? [laughter]

Mack: But I don't want to see us be so egotistical as to believe that students don't do that, and I think that's where we could find more teaching opportunities. You know, when I feel like I'm in the "them vs. us" kind of situation with my students, where I'm trying to make them aware of something that they don't seem to be able to understand, where my students are saying, "upward mobility works" and "We're here, and we're going to become millionaires and so just teach us this stuff and let us get on with it because we *are* going to be millionaires, all of us are" and I'm trying to do something different, you know, that is a problem. But I think if I could get into the resistance that they feel, that maybe we could dialogue about our mutual resistance. And get somewhere with it.

Berlin: Yeah, see my students resisted my attempts to introduce this cultural critique, in the same way that Cy's did, and I finally decided that was a victory because it would have been easy for them to play along with me. And they said, "No, I'm not going to." And it may be the first time they ever said, "No, I'm not going to; I'm not going to play along with you." And so it created a kind of crisis in your life, but it's, you know, awful to say, "I really succeeded today, dear, they all hate me." [laughter]

Knoblauch: Our students spend their whole careers adjusting to different kinds of games.

Mack: Mmmhmm.

Berlin: Yeah, right.

Knoblauch: And how is this different from the other games? I mean it... technically, it's different because the politics of the game are different. Past that, from a student's vantage point, the stakes are the same.

Berlin: Well —

Knoblauch: What do we get from it?

Mack: The grades —

Knoblauch: Well, we get A B C from it, that's what we get.

Berlin: Yeah, but —

Knoblauch: In the context of other things.

Berlin: But the fact of race, class, and gender really makes a difference. I mean the successes in my class are with women [who suddenly realize that] those guys who are trying "to score" with [them are] modeling these masculine truisms about the world according to...the macho, and [they] are saying, "That's stupid." And it problematizes the way [each has] of relating to each other. I mean, it goes beyond the classroom, so —

Reid: I'm hearing two directions here. I'm hearing the direction that the societal structures impose upon people, and then I'm hearing the other direction: the student and other people resisting that. Is that what we want? I mean, is that right? I mean, true, beautiful, whatever? [laughter]

Berlin: Well, it seems to me that our students are convinced that they are unified, coherent, sovereign selves who make decisions about everything, and what I'm trying to do is to get them to realize that most of the decisions have been set up for them. I mean, they don't really have a choice. The whole thing's rigged. They walk around saying, "I really am unique. I really am individual." But their individualities are within acceptable frameworks, so — it is exactly the larger cultural context, the larger semiotic and the individual. I don't want to make them believe that they can be individual; I just want them to understand that they are coded. They're at the center of this whole thing. I mean, we all set up our whole...all of us who are parents, set up our whole lives to code these kids. [laughter]

[pause]

Reid: But is that fair [to] what your definition was earlier, Jim [Zebroski], that's — ok?

Mack: Well, you know, that's one theme: the students not being able to feel comfortable with this, that is a thread through a lot of people's essays, and I have to tell the joke about the Marxist graduate student who said that the highest compliment was her student saying, "I can't enjoy anything anymore after your class." Like for instance, we started off with talking about class in a recent course that I'm teaching, and we read some things about poverty and my students said, "Well, we're really tired of reading about poverty. We know it's — it's ugly." But at the end of the course when I asked them to write letters of complaint, one of the issues that they wanted to focus on was their poverty in relationship to the bookstore. So they wanted to get mad at the bookstore that was making all this money off of them, which they felt wasn't fair. And then they wanted to actually fight with the bookstore. Then they discovered that they really should be mad at a larger group than the bookstore, that the people who worked in the bookstore weren't wealthy—it was the publishers. But you see, then they could get into the issue of wealth. But when I was confronting them with ugly images of poverty, the only thing they could do was say things like "Well, don't these people know about birth control?" and "It's their fault. It's their fault. They could be a Horatio Alger story if they wanted to, they're just not trying." You know, "They're doing it on purpose, being poor." So—I wonder sometimes how abrasive we are in our trying to dialogue about resistance with our students [when] it doesn't get anywhere. I think that they are resistant. I think we need to pay more attention to the ways that they resist.

Berlin: The larger system, not us, but—

Mack: Yeah, yeah, the larger system.

Berlin: You see, what you just said reminded me of the example in your [Knoblauch's] piece about the students who read the story and said—or seven or eight of them who interpreted the thing in terms of upward mobility and these people's failure—do you think any of them could have arrived at a different kind of interpretation?

Knoblauch: I don't think so. I mean not in a meaningful way. I think, if I had wanted to insist on it, they would have said—[laughter]

2

Critical Teaching and Dominant Culture

C. H. Knoblauch

My students come, arguably, from the comfortable middle of the American middle class. I'm as comfortable as they are. My students are white, as I am, their heritage European and Judeo-Christian, as mine is. They are predominantly from a suburban culture, not unlike mine, and many of them, perhaps most, have grown up without substantial experience of people different from themselves. More than half have spent their formative years in the tranquil neighborhoods of Long Island, New York; they drive their own cars between home and school on typical weekends. My students have an average combined SAT score of around 1150. Large numbers of them come to the university expecting to major in Business; most of the rest anticipate professional work in industry, medicine, law, the usual. Our English Department has over 1000 majors (in a population of 12,000 undergraduates), not because the humanities are intrinsically appealing but because the Business School restricts its enrollment and the word is out that English is a good preparation for business and professional careers. The university has a 12 percent "minority" representation among its undergraduates, substantially higher than the "minority" representation among its faculty. Occasionally, the university mounts efforts to recruit from groups outside its mainstream, but it has not been very successful.

My students belong to what the educational Left would call the "dominant culture," a misleadingly simple fiction, to be sure, but one helpfully evocative of the privileges attending those in the United States today who are (sub)urban-white, upper middle-class, Eurocentric in outlook, and either male or willing to accommodate the norms of patriarchal reality. My school has been substantially shaped by that

12

culture, in turn supporting and replicating its values. I too have been constituted in its terms, and I help the school, even when I would prefer not to, in furthering its social and economic agendas. For the most part, not surprisingly, my students accept without self-consciousness the values that their home and school lives have commended to them. They believe that their prosperity is a function of natural merit matched with achievement, through hard work, in the competitive academic marketplace. They believe that the disadvantages of others result from natural limitations (which schooling has effectively "measured"), compounded not infrequently by laziness. They are confident that they deserve to be tomorrow's managers, though more anxious than they really need to be about the success that almost inevitably awaits them. They are also generally quite hostile to the idea that anyone who has not "achieved" as much as they have should be given "unfair" entry to the managerial hierarchy, or even the collegiate training ground, that their own superior effort has merited.

My students accept the stories about freedom and self-actualization, fair play and altruism, progress and prosperity that their history books have composed to portray the American experience. In accepting them they are not more naive than their parents or their teachers. They believe that Abraham Lincoln and Martin Luther King together emancipated black people, so that any disparity between black and white today results from causes other than the merely historical evil of racial prejudice. Many believe — with the Supreme Court — that equal opportunity is a liberal euphemism for reverse discrimination. My women students, no less than the men, believe that the patriarchal oppression of 20, 200, and 2000 years ago (the eras all run together) has given way, conveniently within the last ten years or so, to gender equality, due to the efforts of Jane Fonda and a few other tastelessly but opportunely insistent older women. They believe that their challenge is now to measure up to their male counterparts (whose standards they do not question) according to the neutral scale of merit that properly insures quality control in the workplace. My students have heard about oppression in other parts of the world, a natural consequence of dictatorship, communism, and Islamic religious fervor, but its unfortunate existence does not serve as a call for interference elsewhere and still less as a call for self-scrutiny at home. Nor does it imply any responsibility to open our borders to "aliens" whose presence here might jeopardize the prospects of "our own" people. This is not to imply that my students are selfish or cynical: they are in fact generous, warm-hearted, and sympathetic to others, provided there is no specific threat to their own well-being and perceived entitlements. They are honest and likeable people. They resemble their parents and their teachers.

Nothing in this profile seems peculiar to the situation in my school. It could be substantially replicated for the majority of universities across the country, and indeed for many of the nation's children, whether in college or not. There are, to be sure, other kinds of students and educational settings: grade and high schools serving the underclasses of urban as well as rural poor; trade schools and community colleges comprised of working-class students, many of whom are adults; neighborhood training centers and other nontraditional academic arrangements. There are also different kinds of students within universities, students from diverse cultures, students with working-class and other backgrounds, students whose instincts are liberal, even radical, despite their socioeconomic standing. But several points require emphasis. One is that university life preponderantly reflects the values and expectations of the dominant culture: it is a managerial training ground for the social elite. A second is that university research and curricular agendas have a powerful role in rationalizing, if not actually accounting for, educational realities in other school settings, so that the values of the dominant culture are effectively transmitted to other populations. A third, following partly on the second, is that more people accept those values than just the statistical minority who are readily identified with social privilege. The dominant culture defines how The Good Life is led, not only through its control of schools and other sites of political authority but also through its control of popular media, where images of what constitutes The Good Life offer illusions of possibility to anyone with access to a television, a radio, a magazine, or a movie theater. Where The Good Life does not exist as social reality, it exists as an aspiration concretized through the manipulations of mass culture.

I offer this profile of my students in order to resituate the idea of "critical" or "radical" teaching on atypical and problematic ground: the circumstances of middle-class life familiar to many, if not the majority of, American teachers, even when their classes include students from other backgrounds. Critical teaching, as defined by such educators as Paulo Freire, Henry Giroux, and Ira Shor, seeks to ground the educational enterprise in a cultural and political reflectiveness, shared by teachers and students alike, that enables liberatory action in the face of oppressive social conditions. Historically, critical teaching has emerged in connection with literacy programs in countries, especially in Latin America and Africa, where conditions of profound illiteracy have helped to maintain a ruling elite to the evident detriment of other groups. Activist teachers working with oppressed populations — Freire in Brazil for instance — have been able to illustrate, and make students conscious of, sharp distinctions between rich and poor, landlord and peasant, owner and dispossessed. Typically, when American teachers have appropriated the practices of "critical" pedagogy, they have done so in the name of students perceived to be on the margins of school life, those in remedial programs, those from "minority" groups traditionally excluded from fast academic tracks, those who have dropped out of school. The goal has been to find ways to enfranchise "outsiders," typically by making them more aware of the social realities that constitute their lives; more aware of the means by which power is gained, used, and distributed in the professional and other communities they may wish to enter; more aware of the ways simultaneously to acquire that power and also subvert the structures that objectify prevailing, and debilitating, power arrangements. Shor's efforts in the community college setting and Kozol's in community-based literacy projects are examples.

These are noble enterprises, but they are by no means invariably clear about the precise aims of liberatory education or the concrete praxis, the modes and means of resistance, that ought to characterize critical teaching in the specific circumstances of American life. Who is to be liberated from what? Who gets to do the liberating? Is the U.S. government an oppressor in the same sense that the South African government is? Are middle-class black persons as "outside" as underclass Hispanic? Is Elizabeth Dole an outsider? Where exactly is the inside? Is the goal to make the outsider into an insider? Is it to transform one inside into another? Is it to abolish capitalism? Does the moral commitment, and the political authority, of the critical teacher properly mandate a change in the consciousness of arguably disenfranchised students regardless of their own wishes, their own sense of what they might gain or lose from accommodating themselves to the dominant culture? Since American life does not readily resolve into conflicting images of the hacienda and the mud hut (though it has its versions of both), since profound illiteracy is less common here than in some places, since an alternative literacy in mass media and the myths they propagate is very high indeed, even among so-called outsiders, since most Americans possess reassuring fragments of The Good Life, these questions are not simple. No less complex are the supplementary questions I want to pose in light of the fact that my students belong to the dominant culture, not to the margins by any definition. Is critical teaching anything more than an intellectual game in such circumstances? If not, what does it entail, how is it justified, what are the terms of its success in classrooms filled with literate, economically privileged, young suburbanites, whose political consciousness, in fall, 1988, at least, extended only as far as the wearing of George Bush campaign buttons to class? Are these heirs to American wealth and power in fact the oppressor (re)incarnate, already too corrupted for Freirean dialogue since they have so much to gain from not listening? Can the university really serve as a site for radical teaching? What is the meaning of "radical teacher" for faculty in such privileged institutions—paid by the capitalist state, protected from many of the obligations as well as consequences of social action by the speculativeness of academic commitment, engaged in a seemingly trivial dramatization of utopian thought, which the university itself blandly sponsors as satisfying testimony to its own open-mindedness?

An example will concretize these questions. Last semester I taught English 122, an introduction to shorter prose fiction. My over-enrolled class of forty-three included one Asian student and one black student. The latter, a woman, said nothing all semester, though the class was designed, through small- and large-group formats, to stimulate talk. The ironies of her mute presence haunt my recollection. I followed many of Shor's suggestions for a radical pedagogy, helping students reconstruct the ideological conditions surrounding the production of "literary" texts, involving them in debate, through talk and extensive writing, about the sociocultural tensions and struggles in their own lives by appeal to the mediating situations depicted in stories (*Critical Teaching* 220 ff.). Much of the classwork was technically successful: these students know the drill, know how to interpret, know about foreshadowing and plot and symbol, understand the conventions of literary chatter. At the same time, their readings of stories, their commitment to those readings even in the face of occasional resistance from me or from a few recalcitrant peers, spoke volumes about their own social standing and expectations. We read Toni Cade Bambara's "The Lesson," for instance, a story depicting the experiences of several black children from Harlem who travel to Manhattan, in the company of an adult mentor, Miss Moore, to visit F.A.O. Schwartz, the outrageously upscale toy store. Importantly, the narrator of the story is not an omniscient onlooker, and not even Miss Moore; it is one of the children, Sylvia, an obstreperous youngster who would much rather be swimming, who stiffs the cabbie bringing them downtown in order to keep Miss Moore's money, and who has no inclination at all to learn whatever it is this earnest adult is bent on teaching.

The children, Sylvia included, are awed by what they see, particularly by a toy sailboat that costs over a thousand dollars. They talk about what it might mean that some people spend more on a toy than others have to spend in a year for eating and sleeping. Various opinions are offered. "White folks crazy." "Equal chance to pursue happiness means an equal crack at the dough." But whatever the lesson is, Miss Moore doesn't spell it out for the children, nor do the children agree among themselves. Arguably, Sylvia, the narrator, grasps even less of it than others do. And so the question arises, what do readers think it is? A sampling of the initial written responses I requested from my students is revealing. "I think the lesson Miss Moore was trying to get across was that black people can be smart or rich if they work at it." "When the kids saw the tremendous prices for little toys, they got a sense of money and what it's like to be rich. In other words, if they studied or someway made it out of the slums, they could have such toys." "If you strive for what you want, you can receive it." "The children are living a lifestyle much different than those who are wealthy. Sometimes I got the feeling that the children were jealous of rich and white people." "There's rich and poor and there's ghetto and Park Avenue. You have to work your way up there to get what you want and be what you want." "They can voice their indignation at how the cost of one toy boat could feed an entire family, or they can become educated so as to afford that boat one day."

These responses are too predictable, too understandable, for me to suggest that anyone should be shocked at their middle-class innocence. In any case, the substance of critical teaching does not lie in a co-opting of student readings in favor of one that is, presumably, more socially, ethically, or politically sensitive — namely, the teacher's. Nor does it lie in a mere juxtaposition of opposed readings, with the (naive) hope that students will "see" the merit in some over that in others. Freire observes that "one has to respect the levels of under-standing that those becoming educated have of their own reality. To impose on them one's own understanding in the name of their liberation is to accept authoritarian solutions as ways to freedom" (41). Giroux makes a similar but expanded point. The teacher does not set out to win converts to a personal ideology, even if it has to do with the evils of sexism or racism, through the manipulation of text as moral exhor-tation. To do so is to assume "an authoritative discourse which disallows the possibility for the students to tell their own stories, to present and then question the experiences they bring into play" (*Literacy* 19). Such an abuse of power, whether overt as lecture or disguised as "discussion," replicates the very structures of authority that the radical teacher aims to call into question, resulting either in students' disengaged assent for survival's sake or their sullen resistance.

Critical teaching begins, in this case, not with a power struggle over preferable readings, but with the *reading* of those readings, con-textualized by the life experience of those who produced them. Teacher and students alike engage in self-scrutiny as joint participants in the processes of teaching and learning. I copied several responses to "The Lesson" on the blackboard, asking about the values implicit in the judgments we reached. Certain themes emerged from the talk. Running through these responses, for instance, is a belief that education is intrinsically liberating and also a belief that hard work leads inevitably to The Good Life. Why do we take these as true? If they are true for us, are they then true for everyone? Are they, in fact, always true for us? What does experience suggest? What documentation can we discover? Finally, can we re-enter the story (since it introduces, at least potentially, some exotic "voices" in our conversation) to find alternative meanings, presuming that the scrutiny of our own beliefs has yielded problematic awarenesses of ourselves that the story itself can now serve to interrogate? Can we establish a critical dialogue between our own biographies and the voices of the text? Can we recompose our biographies by means of that critical effort?

The answer might have been yes, given sufficient time and trust, given more courage on both sides. But I was obliged to confront the fact that students are not prepared in school to recognize a dialectical relationship between states of belief and acts of reading, where two sets of meanings interact to produce altered understanding. Instead, they are socialized to presume that the meanings of stories serve to ratify beliefs. Stories are taught in school, from early grades, in order to convey moral messages; they are not supposed to call a dominant morality into question. When they do, they are immoral themselves. My students diligently constructed the usual messages they expected this story to provide, as they had done often before. They agreed, sportingly, to look hard at their values. They made some verbal adjustments to de-emphasize the class bias implicit in their initial pieties about hard work and getting an education. They even produced a new reading of the story—which upheld the very beliefs they had started with, only clothed (as students apparently guessed I wanted them to be) in the trappings of American liberalism. The final, dismissive reading went something like this: in America every child deserves the same opportunity to purchase a thousand-dollar toy sailboat. Students did not want to address the issue of conspicuous consumption that the story invited them to consider; they felt intensely uncomfortable at the suggestion that class differences might be anything but superficial and finally surmountable with hard work; they could not imagine questioning the value system that produces an F.A.O. Schwartz in the first place. Despite the fact that many of them could no more afford a toy from this store than Sylvia or Sugar could, they fought for their psychological investment in its importance as a symbol of The Good Life.

Other stories we discussed produced similar dismissals, similar defeats of oppositional images at the hands of deeply embedded commitments. They decided that the mother in O'Connor's "Everything that Rises Must Converge" is indeed a bigot, but that her son, Julian, having received a college education, is an enlightened man (he isn't) who rightly embarrasses her for her views. They did not consider their own self-righteousness in so easily condemning the mother. They believed that Mrs. Ames, in Boyle's "The Learned Astronomer's Wife," wins her liberation upon discovering that only some men are dreamers like her husband (who ignores her), that others are practical like the plumber (who pays condescending attention to her), and to that extent validations of her own character and abilities. Most students pitied the woman in Tillie Olson's "I Stand Here Ironing" too much to hold her accountable for her daughter's unhappiness; but they levelled aggressive criticism at her for being so irresponsible as to have more children than her economic condition allowed. They concluded that the Arab, in Camus' "The Guest," goes to prison on his own, despite Daru's gift of a "choice" to return to his own people, because he respects the value of (French colonial) law and feels a (Western) obligation to Daru, who has placed him "on his honor."

The issue here seems to go beyond tactics to a question of the real plausibility of liberatory teaching in circumstances where there is a powerful self-interest, rooted in class advantage, that works actively, if not consciously, against critical reflectiveness. What do my students have to gain from a scrutiny of values and conditions that work to insure their privilege? Why should they struggle with the troubling self-awareness that one course aims to create when the culture of the university as a whole reassures them of their entitlements? Shor makes some pragmatic but discouraging concessions. Since teachers can only create the conditions of democratic learning, cannot compel assent to a radical agenda (except at cost to the very democracy they seek to establish), there are real boundaries to what critical teaching can accomplish. The "consciousness in each class" will determine "the limits of egalitarian reconstruction." Moreover, "in each school or college, teachers need to assess what level of liberatory learning they can assert, given student consciousness and institutional politics." Shor's postscript to this debilitating admission is that "students are a mass of potential allies" because they have, finally, "the most to gain by the success of democratic learning" (112–13). But Shor's students are working-class adults in the community college, whose interests are not well served by their capitulation to the dominant culture, whose discovery of critical consciousness might be an enabling step in reconstituting their social reality. What do my students have to gain?

The question is a serious one, to which moral pieties will not serve as adequate response. But its difficulty must not imply an invitation to university teachers to accept the comfortable disengagement of fatalism, leaving the issue of educational transformation to those alone who work with marginalized populations. Giroux warns that applying the project of critical teaching restrictively to contexts of the disadvantaged and dispossessed falsely conceives of literacy in terms of a "deficit theory of learning." Schools, the reasoning goes, "unevenly distribute particular skills and forms of knowledge" in ways that benefit the middle class, and so the aim of radical pedagogy is merely to insure that outsiders get the reading and writing skills necessary to live critically in the school world and eventually to gain economic equality. In this view, literacy becomes "privileged cultural capital," with "minority" students deserving their fair piece of the pie. What this argument produces is a parochial, functionalist concept of literacy that ignores any pervasive commitment to name and transform "ideological and social conditions that undermine the possibility for forms of community and public life organized around the imperatives of a critical democracy." Composing such a democracy is not a matter of turning outsiders into insiders: it entails a pervasive, ceaseless, public negotiation of power arrangements in the interest of social justice; it implies the necessary participation of "those members of the middle and upper classes who have withdrawn from public life into a world of sweeping privatization, pessimism, and greed" (*Literacy* 5).

I don't have a fully adequate answer to the question of what advantage my students might expect from the development of social responsibility. But I have reason to believe that a portrait of middle-class, upwardly mobile suburbanites consumed by nothing more than self-interest and opportunism would be a dishonest caricature, unresponsive to the complexities of life. My students are self-interested, but they are not only that. They do seek The Good Life, but not at any cost. They cling to their myths, but they also learn and change. Perhaps that is the starting point for reconsidering the plausibility of critical teaching in the university setting. There is a tendency to assume that its challenge is to overcome an inertial condition, but that assumption is false. Change, not stasis, is the condition of life: the instructional challenge, accordingly, is not to force open obstinately closed minds, but to intervene creatively in processes of change that are already underway, making use of the intellectual disequilibrium that the university can foster in the interest of learning. There is also a tendency to assume monolithic conditions surrounding the enterprise of critical teaching: "students of the dominant culture" is such a monolith when conceived not as a helpful analytic abstraction but as a fact of social life. The university is as much a contested ground as other institutions are, one where alternative goals and methods, liberal, conservative, and radical agendas, teachers and students from assorted backgrounds are the stuff of dialectic. Any classroom is a site of conflicting beliefs, values, affiliations, desires, class and gender identities, the tapping of which can offer opportunity for critical reflection. There were moments of such opportunity, brief but potent, in my own class: women who felt authentic fear and anger after reading Lessing's "A Woman on the Roof," people arguing about the chauvinist narrator's prejudices in implying Margaret's murderous intent in "The Short Happy Life of

Francis Macomber," students puzzled and frustrated over the paradoxical values in Singer's "Gimpel the Fool," students appalled at the money/success ethic behind the tragedy in Lawrence's "A Rocking-Horse Winner." It may be that the rewards of critical teaching must always be found in such small, tantalizing moments of classroom encounter, not in measurable advances on the grand schemes that theoretically propel the enterprise. Whether the accumulation of those details is likely in the end to add up to the realizing of those schemes constitutes one of the many uncertainties, the many hopes or doubts that teachers learn, and ought to learn, to live with.

Works Cited

Freire, Paulo, and Donaldo Macedo. *Literacy: Reading the Word and the World*. Introduction by Henry Giroux. South Hadley, MA: Bergin & Garvey, 1987.

Shor, Ira. *Critical Teaching and Everyday Life*. Chicago: U of Chicago, 1987.

Berlin: Only 19 percent of the work force are college graduates. I mean most of the kids that we deal with aren't going to make it, right? I mean it's...is that true? Is it that bad? I think, yeah—

Zebroski: I would go one step further, Jim, I'd say that we, no less than our students, in fact perhaps a great deal more, buy into the images of the good life. And that for us to take on the guilt for the system is really kind of crazy. *Because* it seems to me, compared to Donald Trump who may not be even among the top few people in the country with power and wealth, I clearly have little in common. There are probably not a whole lot of really very wealthy people, I mean people with a great deal of power. I may be wrong, but I don't think anyone here teaches at Harvard or Yale. Those kinds of schools are often the places where you might encounter that, and you only get there if you're already in it—

Mack: Right, exactly—

Zebroski: So, I teach this stuff because I'm thinking about these very things for myself, and I want to share that with my students. I don't want to impose it on 'em. But, you know, I have some questions about my place in this system, and I don't feel the need to take on the guilt of the oppressor at all. I feel certain constraints just as my students do.

Reid: So what's the goal of this, of education, of asking students to resist in— helping them to understand the structures and the political structures so that they can resist—is the goal greater control of their own lives, or is, the goal social reform? And if the goal is social reform, who are we to say—

Stuckey: What it is—

Reid: What it is—

Stuckey: Oh, hell! I can talk all day about what social reform is—

Reid: Well, sure! Sure. All of us can—

Singleton: Well, now I don't—

Reid: But I mean it sounds to me like we're talking about two completely different goals. I mean I'm not—

Zebroski: But they're parts of each other—

Reid: I have students who are already—

Zebroski: They're really caught up in each other—

Mack: Yeah.

Zebroski: If I have sort of a narrative of individual satisfaction, and I say, "Oh this social stuff's nice, but I really don't want to deal with it for whatever useful or rational reasons," that narrative is part of that social stuff. In some ways, it's easy for me not to do this political stuff in the classroom. And yet, in some ways, for the full development of the individual, I think you need a fuller development of society. I think those things are very closely connected. I mean—

Reid: I can see how those are interrelated, but I have plenty of students who are perfectly unhappy already without my help—

Zebroski: Well—

Reid: And out of control, and with no control over their lives—

Berlin: Right, right.

Reid: And I don't know why I should make them more unhappy.

Zebroski: I'm not saying that—

Berlin: Well, the thing is we [university professors] have happy kids, see. [laughter] We have the nice...you know, they're going to make it somehow.

Mack: But I like the word *narrative* that Jim brought up, and I think I got that mostly from Marian Yee's article about the narrative—just by growing up in this culture, that there are only certain narratives—you [Berlin] used the word *image*—that are allowable, that are acceptable, and what I'd like to do is to help them to see that they could create a different narrative, but [that] this narrative is not an individual narrative. See, in a way, that would totally ruin the whole Horatio Alger [story], you know, "I will succeed as an individual, and the system works if I can as an individual be successful." I want them to make a narrative that will be a social act. That would be my ultimate hope for my students, that they would take the authority to create a different narrative.

3

Are You the Teacher?

Marian Yee

At the threshold of the doorway, I feel like the understudy who's been called up at the last moment to perform in place of the real actor, and who, never believing this moment would come, had never fully learned the lines. The space I have to cross is not so wide — a step takes me into the classroom and into my role as "teacher." But I always have the sense on these first-day-of-class entrances that the other side eludes me.

Even after I have crossed the threshold and stand looking over the seated students from the head of the classroom, I'm still not sure that I'm in the right place. From our respective positions we feel out our parts: English teacher and college students. As always, I wonder, as I go over the attendance and shuffle my official handouts, whether I will get The Question. Sometimes it comes; sometimes it doesn't. Sometimes it hovers, unasked, over the desks; sometimes a wise-mouthed student, or just an unwitting one, will snap it out like the sudden, sharp burst of gum: "Are you the teacher?"

"Are you the teacher?" *Am* I? *The gap at the threshold widens.* I suppose that any of a number of factors might have prompted this question: I don't look old enough to be an authority figure; I don't look big enough to be "the boss"; or I'm not the "right" race for this subject. I can sympathize with their confusion; after all, I had never in my high school or undergraduate training encountered an English teacher who looked like me. The image of a Chinese woman teaching English was as foreign to me as it probably is to my Composition 101 students. The gap is the space opened up between "you" and "teacher."

Who is this "you" that they are looking at? Who is the "teacher"? What images, associations separate the two? Do Chinese women inhabit a different sphere than English teachers? What are those spheres like?

How do we know about them? From whose point of view do we see them? When I try to picture an "English teacher" I see someone like Professor Kingsfield on *Paper Chase*. Although he is a law professor in this movie and not an English teacher, he epitomizes The Teacher in its classic form as the holder of knowledge and power. This image is perpetuated in the character of a more recent popular movie: Professor Keating in *Dead Poets Society*. Whether he is distant and exclusive or radical and inspiring, the teacher as holder of knowledge and power incites hero worship and tends to inhabit the form of a white man. These are not the only images I have of teachers, however; they compete with others: the woman in my high school, a single mother of three children, who taught poetry workshops after school. She introduced me to poems I had never read in the classroom before, poems written by men and women who weren't dead. There are teachers like Jaime Escalante, the Hispanic math teacher who inspired his students at East Los Angeles's Garfield High and was powerfully portrayed by Edward James Olmos in the movie *Stand and Deliver*. But even given the range of diverse models of English teachers available, my students' first visual association with that category is probably closer to a Professor Kingsfield than to someone like me.

When I think of "Chinese women" I think of small, dark-haired women like my mother and her friends, who work as seamstresses in sweatshops. Or I think of silky, red women with talons for nails: steamy dragon-ladies from kung-fu movies. Or I remember the yellow-colored people with slanted eyes and long pigtails in book illustrations. In my own experience, English teachers and Chinese women have occupied mutually exclusive categories; these characters have stories that take them in different directions. While this has not prevented me from becoming an English teacher, these inherited, iconographic stories have shaped the way I, and apparently my students, tend to perceive myself in this role.

Sometimes the uneasiness I feel when I walk into a classroom on the first day is so strong that I am surprised the students don't get up at once and walk out, refusing to accept me as their teacher. However, they always sit there expectantly, pencils poised, so that I am sometimes deceived into thinking that they do not notice any difference in me. I'm reminded of a story that my friend Fatima, a Filipino woman, once told me. Her first day of class ritual begins with an anonymous entry. She chooses a seat at the back of the classroom and watches as students file in for their English class. When everyone is settled and waiting for the teacher to arrive, she gets up, walks to the front of the class and starts calling attendance. This is her favorite moment of the term: she loves to watch their jaws drop. Obviously, then, students do notice and are always quick to notice differences. But while my friend chooses to deliberately call attention to her difference, my impulse is usually to hide it behind my authority. When I have gotten The Question, I have deflected it with a piece of chalk: I turn to the blackboard and print "Marian Yee," pretending that what they are really asking is "What is your name?" And with this official, white-lettered sign between us, and without further explanation except when my office hours are, The Question gets dropped. Class begins, the gap is closed. For I have learned this: I don't ever have to answer this question. Though the signs of difference compete with the signs of authority, in a socially indoctrinating institution like the university, the signs of authority usually win.

What I want to consider now is how the "you" gets reabsorbed into "teacher." Evidently, the categories we tend to place things in are not necessarily static or exclusive. Movements can take place between categories: a Chinese woman can be an English teacher, and vice versa. Indeed, the tenets of a liberal, humanist education decree that who "you" are shouldn't matter since "teacher" only designates a specified professional role. "You" occupy this role within a specific setting and can occupy other roles within other settings. Thus, "you" as a student in a college English class can occupy a different role from that which "you" occupy in your family, church, club, or other community. These liberal tenets safeguard that my being a member of a certain community (the Chinese community, say) will not disqualify or prevent me from being part of another community (for example, the academic community).

But what happens when these communities come into conflict; when, for example, the values of home contend with what is taught at school; when communities compete for the authority to define who "you" are? It is true that I can simultaneously be a Chinese woman and an English teacher (and many other things), but the fact that this union appears to some to be an uneasy one indicates that the movement between communities and between categories is not an unproblematic one. *Are you the teacher?*

What makes the migration between the categories of "Chinese women" and "English teacher" problematic? Historically and socially, the immigration of Asians to America has not been an easy one; the distance between countries and between cultures was crossed with great difficulty. Yet the story of our arrival and adjustment is usually told as a narrative of successful assimilation. As this story goes, these people were once outsiders, but then they became Americanized; they were able to overcome their cultural differences in order to belong. I think of my father, who has found only part-time work delivering newspapers since the restaurant that he worked in for twenty years went out of business. Or my mother, who recently explained to me how she had practiced her English to ask her boss for a raise and ended up telling him that she was making "too much money." Adjustment for them means putting away the chopsticks and taking out cutlery once a year for the Thanksgiving meal. Meanwhile, the Chinese New Year is no longer a family celebration since the school and work calendar have made it hard to take time to come home to eat a meal my mother would have spent days preparing.

Materially, they are undeniably better off than they were in China. However, the home they have found and made in the United States since they emigrated here is not one where they are able to be truly at home. Part of their discomfort is the inevitable result of relocating from a familiar place and way of life to a totally alien one. But this discomfort is an important aspect of their experience that is not told in an assimilation narrative, which dominates the description of the immigrant experience in America as a process of belonging. The form of the dominant assimilation narrative does not allow any expressions of ambivalence or resistance to the process of cultural loss that may accompany the process of belonging. In fact, loss is not part of that story: becoming Americanized is seen as a desirable end and as a gain.

Narratives pervade our lives; they are the commonplace stories that facilitate explanations of where and how things belong in our culture. As readily available forms that describe the meaning of our experiences, cultural narratives operate as powerful definers of what we ought to feel or value. In order to resist them, we must first understand how cultural narratives work and how they are used. As I have pointed out, cultural narratives tend to simplify complex experiences by suppressing other narratives that might express conflict, contradictions, or ambivalence. In doing so it presents as coherent what is actually being contested. For example, the assimilation narrative addresses the concerns of groups in competition for cultural as well as physical space. The outcome of this competition, within the terms of the assimilation narrative, is that the outsider group gradually loses its foreign characteristics and adapts to the values and outlook of the native group. The boundaries this narrative creates serve to establish a story of origin and centrality for one group and marginal affiliation for the other group. "Native" and "foreigner" are terms that try to persuade you to accept certain limits. If this cultural narrative were historically accurate, we would have stories about how the colonizing Europeans adapted to the customs, rituals, and values of the Native Americans. But the fact is that power, rather than historical accuracy, is the goal of an assimilation narrative; power in this sense is the ability to create and perpetuate narratives that define who or what is inside, and who or what is outside.

The entry of Chinese immigrants into America reveals the contradictions of this narrative as applied to the Asian-American experience. Asians were a valuable labor resource at a time when America was rapidly expanding. Their work on railroad and mining projects helped to connect and develop the vast western territory for settlement and trade. However, they themselves represented a threat to the space they were helping to open up: they were not simply temporary imported workers, but permanent occupants of this land, competing with whites for the right to inhabit the new country. That right was largely denied, however, because citizenship was denied to them. Tough immigration laws directed at the Chinese to control their entry into America were accompanied by popular narratives that warned of the "Yellow Peril": the story of how hordes of Asians were posed to invade the country. The assimilation narrative and the Yellow Peril narrative are not different stories. Read in the context of the Yellow Peril narrative we can see that an assimilation narrative is a story about how to make difference safe by making it more like the dominant culture.

In order to begin retelling our own stories, we need to recognize the way that popular stories have characterized us. Having grown up in this country, I am the product of the assimilation narrative. I am also a product of the Yellow Peril narrative. I remember experiencing this dual heritage vividly in the second grade once. I was rewarded for my docility by being selected to run an errand for the teacher. In the hallway I encountered another student, a little boy, who was perhaps on a similar mission. When he saw me, he pulled down the corners of his eyes and pelted me with hard, ugly sounds, lashing out with all the "ching chong" words he knew. So while I experience all the advances and awards of a well-trained student, at the same time, when I walk into the classroom and feel uncomfortable and different, I realize the extent to which I've internalized the Asian as "other."

Do my students also feel the tension of conflicting cultural narratives working within them when they react to me? When they ask me if I am the teacher, it seems to me that they are articulating this very tension. Their surprise is not from lack of familiarity with cultural cliches and narratives that would help them "place" me (if anything they are overexposed to such narratives). But they are uncertain how to read these narratives when the positions of the characters change: when the outsider *is* the insider, the foreigner now the subject, instead of the object to be assimilated. An important aspect of the assimilation narrative they are responding to is the image of the foreigner, which never really disappears in this narrative. If anything, difference is highlighted in order to emphasize a story about crossing social boundaries (despite the "handicap" of difference) in which the actual "arrival" always refers back to the distance traversed rather than the situated present.

It is not surprising, then, for my students to be confused. But behind that confusion is something else — an unarticulated *anxiety*. How *do* you arrive? If literacy is supposed to provide the traveler with his or her passport, then students in their first college composition class must feel the tenuousness of their positions. First-year college students feel acutely how uninitiated they are in institutional forms of expression. From writing an essay for an English class to interacting with other students at a fraternity party, they struggle to learn their "place" while wondering what place there will be for them if they don't fit in. Instead of being a reassuring figure who illustrates that difference can be assimilated, I appear to disrupt that narrative. When they ask me if I am the teacher, on the one hand they have "misread" the assimilation narrative, but on the other hand, they have read it only too accurately by reacting to its internal contradictions.

One way to respond to their question is to acknowledge it as a process of reading. Reading in this sense is the practice of attending to the conflicts, contradictions, and ambiguities in texts. I am a "text" in the sense that I represent a particular group that is publicly inscribed within powerful cultural narratives. The point, however, is not to correct these narratives. The process of rejecting one narrative and replacing it with another will not give me or my students a truer or more complete account of who I am or of who they are. It is necessary for me to hold many narratives within me at once, for I am composed of many parts. Each student is, himself or herself, composed of multiple narratives that compete with each other to tell the main story.

One way to engage students in this lesson is to return to the name on the board. I might bracket my name in quotation marks, allowing us to step back from "me" for a moment. Then I might invite them to make a list of all the images, associations, stories that come to mind when they think of "me" as a "teacher" or as a "Chinese" "woman." The first assignment for the course might be for them to bracket their own names and construct a similar list in which they explore the stories that describe their roles as students, as men and women, as members of ethnic or racial groups, and so on.

Teaching students how to recognize and read the dominant cultural narratives that construct their identities and their views of the world is a way to help them rethink writing, not as an act of recording those narratives but as acts of resisting and re-evaluating those narratives, and of recovering other narratives that have been suppressed or ignored. Our goal as composition teachers is to help students gain an active voice and critical role in their own composing processes by helping them to create narratives in which their differences need not be obliterated, but instead recognized and respected.

It is important then, not to overlook a question like: Are you the teacher? This is one of the most important questions students can ask, for what they are also asking is: Who am *I* and what does it mean for me to be a *student*? When we engage with this question, when we choose to step into the gap, it may feel like we are falling through the floor. But another way to see this is as an important opportunity to negotiate new ground to stand on. After all, we have nothing to lose but our foundations when we listen to the wise mouthings of our students.

Blitz: Marian's paying attention to the question "Are you the teacher?" for the first time, really noticing the narrative implications of the question, the political implications as well, strike[s] me as really important. This is a question that, if we pay attention to it in the classroom, starts to ring bells outside the classroom. It has a lot to do with who is sleeping outside my building and dying on the subway grating, for instance. And it has a lot to do with my students. Upon discovering that I'm a Jew, [they] say, "You're a Jew?" and suddenly everything is thrown into scary relief for a second.

Yee: I see that there are two problems, then. One is that there's a sense in which I don't want to make a big deal out of it [the question, "Are you the teacher?"] because there are some things about a liberal education that I agree with, such as just because I'm Asian doesn't mean that I can't do this. It doesn't mean that I can't occupy one role and maintain other roles in other situations. On the other hand, I want to explore what the limits of a liberal education are, and how that process of students noticing this difference is a way of testing those limits —

Mack: I really liked your piece because it didn't give answers. I started thinking about myself as a narrative, and in itself it was an important mental gambit for me to consider that, and maybe have my students consider themselves as that. Only I didn't get that far. I'm still dealing with thinking about my being a narrative, that my students read me as a narrative in ways that I don't want. And I know they do, and I'm still trying to think about that.

4

The Names We Resist
Revising Institutional Perceptions of the Nontenured

Donna Singleton

June 15, 1989

To My Readers,

I am one of the growing body of practitioners known by such demeaning terms as *call staff, part-timers, part-time people, hourly staff, lecturers, visiting lecturers,* or *adjuncts.*

My friends and acquaintances outside of the college community are impressed when they learn that I teach at a university. Most of them inaccurately assume such a position carries with it an increase in status and salary compared to high school employment. College students are also generally unaware of the hierarchy that exists in departments. And many "regular" faculty are unaware of the hiring practices and salaries of those in nontenure track positions. Being somewhat new to the college teaching community, I came sharing many of those views.

October 8, 1988

Mark,

I am excited about participating in the book about resistance and see it as a great opportunity because the issues need to be raised. But I am also scared! I fear the possible ramifications of participating. My position teaching basic writing is not very secure. Remember that I am not on a tenure-track. Only last year did I get a nine-month contract even. As I talk with others, I see more clearly the dangers in what I am doing and writing. Could this be really harmful to me? I know how some in our university feel about those who raise issues, who speak out. Will this participation be frowned upon? Should I keep it quiet? Will I be offered another contract? Will participation in this book prevent me from being hired elsewhere? These are real fears.

Also there are ethical considerations. I don't want to feel like a spy or an informant in revealing practices and attitudes. I feel a disloyalty if I discuss out of house the things we all complain about within it. But how can I be loyal to a system if it does not value me? And at the same time, I see there are concerns that will not be addressed if they remain invisible because of tradition or if they are ignored because some assume that there's no need to "make a big deal" over nothing. Also, I have seen that there are some who are making changes. I think I would feel more disloyal if I did not speak out and work for change.

Donna

February 24, 1989

On September 25, 1984, a few days after I became a teaching assistant in the English department, my education in the politics of academia began. In my mailbox — in the bottom row of a hierarchy of mailboxes — I found a copy of a memo to the Provost, the Dean of Humanities, the English Chair, and the English faculty (and copies to Part-time Instructors and Graduate Assistants) from one of the nontenured teachers. The subject was "Title for English Part-time Staff":

> I strenuously object to the term Call Staff and suggest instead either Instructor (part-time, if need be) or Visiting Lecturer (as designated by contracts).
>
> Call Staff is, at best, demeaning, derogatory, suggestive of transience and availability, a downplaying of professionalism (some of these, so called, have earned Ph.D.s, or equivalent, that compete with lesser degrees earned by full-fledged department members fortunate enough to find positions before the employment crunch worsened).
>
> I, personally, will not recognize myself as Call Staff nor consider myself as having been addressed professionally by any member of [the university] who so condescends.

At that point I had not even known that the term *call staff* was regularly used for those who were hired as needed quarter by quarter — sometimes as late as the day before classes were to begin. Needless to say, the memo stirred up some talk. Several of the teachers employed on this basis agreed that the term was degrading and had obvious connotative connections with the term *call girl*. The comparison to one who was expected to wait, ready and willing, for a call at a momentary whim of an authority willing to pay a fee for services rendered was not lost on these teachers.

The memo invoked other reactions. Some people didn't understand "what the big deal was" and shrugged it off with derogatory comments about the author. Some applauded the action and the guts of the protestor. Some, suddenly made aware, were shocked that they had merely accepted the use of the term. The department chair quickly responded, using the term *visiting lecturer* thereafter. Other departments, however, continue to use the term. But even when the name is changed, many of the same attitudes represented by the terminology remain, and many of the other terms are also problematic.

Part-time is a typical designation. The irony of the situation is that many of these dedicated teachers have heavier teaching loads than "full-time" or "regular" faculty. (It should be noted that there are several different groups of people employed on a part-time basis. Wallace [1984] discusses the categories thoroughly. My discussion is based on my experience and is limited to those who want full-time employment. Readers wanting a more comprehensive view should see the references.) A few have nine-month contracts, and some have taught for eight years or more. So why do we continue to use the term *part-time*?

Many universities use the term *adjunct* for this group of teachers. It is interesting to note that the dictionary defines this as "a secondary or nonessential addition" and "attached in a subordinate capacity." Try to imagine what would happen across the country if all these "nonessential" teachers suddenly disappeared. What if department memos came out addressed to "Full-time Faculty, Nonessential Faculty, and Graduate Assistants"?

Lecturer is the term now given to those in our English department who have been given a nine-month contract, and *visiting lecturer* is used for those who are hired quarter by quarter to fill in if additional sections are needed. Either term is something of a misnomer at best.

For example, just after I was hired as a visiting lecturer for the first time, I made this entry in my journal:

> October 26, 1986
> Went to the library to get some books today. First time to use my appointment card rather than my student ID. The young student worker looked at the card and said "Oh, you're a visiting lecturer? Where are you from?" I told her, not thinking much about it till she added, "Well, I hope you enjoy your stay with us."

I could tell that she assumed I was someone who was brought in for a special assignment. She had no idea that "visiting lecturer" meant a person hired quarter by quarter with no benefits, a meager salary, and a restricted appointment — a person considered, by some deans, one of those "dime a dozen" nonessentials. An amusing yet sad incident.

And what of the term *lecturer*? As I worked on this piece, I wrote to Mark Hurlbert about the conflict I felt with the names I am called. *Lecturer* seems inappropriate since I do not lecture; I try to encourage a community of writers within the classroom. I questioned whether *teacher* was appropriate since I encourage students to "teach themselves." Mark responded to my discontent:

> 14 May 1989
>
> You are right to ask, why should I be called a lecturer or visiting lecturer! What informed writing teacher lectures? Why are you only visiting? What sort of commitment does your institution want from you? What do other institutions demand of their "part-timers"? What beliefs, theories, and power structures does it support and perpetuate? We are, I think you have argued, oppressed by the terms applied to us because the terms imply institutional and professional attitudes, reified power structures, artificial and demeaning relationships. You, it seems to me, are resisting the names you are called because you are more than those names and you resent the way they attempt to diminish you.

July 5, 1989

Friends reading this draft today asked some pertinent questions. One wondered what job title I would prefer and noted that he is called "hourly staff" because that is how he is paid. Another offensive term for me. But he did put me on the spot: what name *would* I prefer? Is there an appropriate name? The only term I have felt comfortable using as I discuss this with others is *nontenured*.

Another reader questioned whether the name is the thing since for him the issue was one of pay, tenure, and benefits. I have to say that, of course, pay, tenure, and benefits *do* matter, and I want to see changes there too. But how I am named is important in that it reflects how I am viewed. The language we use to designate and classify serves to define our perceptions and even to *create* or perpetuate those perceptions — and the pay and benefit structure as well. The realization that we have difficulty naming, *entitling* (in all its meanings), this group, now estimated at 40 percent of all composition teachers, is indicative of the pervasive oppressive attitudes.

We encounter our naming (remember the childhood term *name calling*?) primarily through department documents such as memos. When, as a grad student and later when employed part-time, I received memos labeled "To All English Faculty," I felt included. I remember being surprised and wondered if it was a mistake. When, however, I received memos labeled "To all Full-time and Part-time English Faculty and Graduate Assistants," I felt categorized and set aside. I felt put in my place. When I received a memo that listed each person (fifteen of them) by last name in alphabetical order with no distinctions for gender or academic rank (grad students, tenured, and nontenured all thrown in together), I felt I was in a collaborative effort with others doing the same job. I felt I was a colleague. Another memo, from one of the full-time teachers, listed forty-three names as individuals, though they were grouped by category — full-time, part-time, and grad assistant. These last two examples were one person's courtesy toward professional colleagues. "Colleague" — is that the name I want?

I notice that memos to deans and chairs often list the individual names. As the memos filter down to teachers, group names are generally used. I was privy to these memos from higher in the ranks because the department chair chose to conduct a very "open" administration by passing to the entire department many of the directives from the deans and provost. Since I came in under such an administration, I assumed that was the way things were done at this institution. I later learned that it was the philosophy of *that* chair, and the open policy changed with the next election.

Consider the implications of the following memo "salutations": To: All Humanities Faculty; To: English Faculty; To: English Department Colleagues; To: Humanities Colleagues. What do these forms of address say to us? What do they tell us about the relationship between the sender and the recipient? Does the naming change with the intent of the message, whether it is a directive or an announcement? Informal announcements about health or retirement or social events tend to be the "humanities colleagues" type, whereas department policies often carry the hierarchical distinctions.

July 18, 1989

As I reread my draft, I wonder if these are conscious decisions by the administration. Is it the whim of the secretary? The way the last form was done? I remember an old story about a young child who asked her mother why she always cut the roast into two parts before putting it into the pan. The mother said she did it the way her mother had done it. They checked with the grandmother who gave the same reason. Fortunately for the story, the great-grandmother was still alive to solve the mystery. "I did it that way," said Granny, "because my pan was too small." I think the story has relevance here because we need to find out if there is a decision being made and why, and I suppose we need more inquisitive voices saying, "Why do we do it that way?" and "What message are you sending when you do it that way?" Might some perceive that listing each group would be inclusive, not exclusive?

Even a simple document like the department phone roster declares the hierarchy. The five pages begin with three pages of professors, alphabetically arranged, then the alphabetical listing of associate professors, then the group of assistant professors, the instructors, and then the two secretaries. Next, there is a new sheet for the part-time faculty, followed by another page for teaching assistants. If such notation is necessary, couldn't it be noted after the names in one alphabetical list? Like the phone roster, there is a mailbox hierarchy, as noted earlier, with designations at the bottom for part-timers and TA's. We have to know the rank to find phone numbers, mailboxes, and offices. Somehow this allegiance to hierarchy reminds me of military rank and protocol. What can we learn from this association? Where and how do such practices begin? Where do they end?

There are two places in my professional life where this issue of rank or naming is almost nonexistent: in the classroom and at professional conferences. My students tend to assume that I am "regular" faculty, and having no title or rank, I usually give my first and last name and encourage a first-name atmosphere. Occasionally, some students will address a note in their journals to "Professor Singleton, or Dr. Singleton, or is it Donna?" Sometimes they ask about the "etiquette" of the degrees or the titles, or comment on trying to find a name in the mailbox hierarchy, but basically they figure that we are all equal in terms of status and salary. They have other criteria for ranking the faculty.

Even more than in the classroom, I feel removed from the confines of hierarchy at professional conferences—when I can afford to go, of course. Once there, I do not feel marked or categorized. Calls for papers are supposedly open to all and state that they try to include new voices as well as familiar ones on the programs. Conversation tends to center around concepts rather than contracts. Increasing attention is being given to special-interest groups devoted to addressing some of the problems of the nontenured. Basically, I have always felt that my participation is welcomed, no questions asked.

May 10, 1989

As I have been looking at these issues and exploring them, I have been talking with others. My awareness is contagious. I got a call from a colleague telling me of an item I might want to include in my chapter. Department evaluations had been put in all of the mailboxes—blue forms for full-time faculty, pink for part-time. I jotted this in a note to Mark Hurlbert and his response did more than just echo the sentiments of my friends in the department:

June 4, 1989

I have to respond to something you told me about in your letter, namely, the pink and blue forms for department evaluation. Here's just one more example of the kinds of institutional power structures we need to resist. First, as you say, what anonymity exists in a situation where "regular" faculty fill out blue forms and part-timers fill out pink ones? And isn't this an interesting choice of colors? Blue for "boys" — full-timers (is your full-time faculty mostly, as in most English faculties, male?); and pink for "girls" — are most of your part-time writing faculty, as in most English departments, female? And more, by giving you a pink form (pink slip) to fill in aren't they consciously or unconsciously reminding you of your tenuous position in the department — that you could be fired at any minute? We can learn much, it seems to me, about what we ought to work to change in our institutions by studying the semiotics — not to mention the rhetorics — of the documents they give us — as well as those we ourselves disseminate.

Mark's last sentence prompted me to look further. As I looked at the university's documents, I saw that they are just one part of the picture. If they speak and I only listen, there is no dialogue. The names they give me, their memos and other documents are monologic if I do not respond. Those are probably meant to be one-way communiques, top-down directives, aren't they? Is that the difference between a memo and a letter? (The dictionary tells me that a memo, a clipped form of memorandum, is a short note written to remind oneself of something or an informal written communication, as within an office. Is the institution reminding itself? reinforcing itself? Are memos still informal? And why not letters, which imply an answer — *correspondence*, communication by letters.) Again, if I don't respond, there is a monologue and I acquiesce to the directives. If I respond, as did my colleague who refused to be called "call staff," then I force the institution to dialogue with me, though they may respond with silence. There is a German proverb *Keine Antwort ist auch eine Antwort* — No answer is also an answer. And just as much to the point, if *I* do not answer, my lack of an answer *is* an answer of acceptance.

July 17, 1989

Mark,

It occurs to me as I revise this that I have not shared with the department or people involved what I am now sharing with a wider audience! As I have thought about it and searched my files, I have not asked anyone why. No wonder I felt like an informant or spy when I began this close look at naming and resisting. I did not have the courage ("guts" was the first word that came to mind!) to talk to anyone, and here I am writing it for publication. That's not fair. I can't be a closet resister, can I? So, I feel I should write some letters. But how do I explain why? It sounds risky.

How do I resist this temptation to merely accept the status quo? How do I resist the tendency to see myself in the subservient role that the hierarchy has established? Freire speaks of the prescriptive nature of the oppressor/oppressed relationship, the oppressed adhering to the guidelines of the oppressor (31). It seems these memos, not only in their content but in their format, are part of this prescription. And the "part-time" faculty internalize the department guidelines that dictate place, name, role, and voice (or the lack of these) in the hierarchy. But Freire reminds us that "Freedom is acquired by conquest, not by gift. It must be pursued constantly and responsibly" (31). The pursuit requires recognition of the causes of the oppression, accepts the reality of risk taking, and the fear involved in both the risk taking and the achievement of "authentic existence" (32).

Slowly I am becoming aware of the practices that define my existence within the university. And *I* am beginning to see the implications of the names and policies used to define my existence. Now, how do I redefine my existence since I see that, generally, the initiative will not come from the oppressor? In other words, how do I resist? The pursuit must go beyond names and memos to other questions. Who determines grading standards for freshman composition? Who selects the textbooks? Who serves on committees? Who should?

One issue in my school as well as others is the lack of representation for the nontenured faculty on freshman writing committees. These committees make policy decisions that affect all those who teach fresh-man composition, a large percentage of whom were once employed on a part-time basis. As a teaching assistant, I served on such a committee with full voting rights. My voice was heard and respected. The following year, when I was employed as a visiting lecturer, I had no representation on that committee. What does this say of the relative importance of the "part-time" faculty and the graduate student?

In spite of this departmental policy, I have experienced the positive influence of having full-time faculty who are sensitive to the needs and recognize the value of the nontenured faculty. The faculty who train our teaching assistants and who are responsible for the freshman writing program have consistently validated the dedication and expertise of the nontenured. We are encouraged to participate in meetings and decision making. Because of this atmosphere, I came in assuming that I mattered. As I said, I was naively unaware of my "place" as it was defined by some in the administration.

January 26, 1990
At my insistance the developmental department is now represented at meetings of the Freshman Writing Committee, which administers our freshman comp courses, and I learned at a meeting today that finally the by-laws have been changed to have elected representation of the nontenured lecturers!

Such changes must come about. And I have seen how it can come about. It comes from people validating themselves by affirming who they are and what they can do. It starts with refusing a demeaning name and taking the risks to speak out, as my colleague did with the term *call staff*. It means being informed. When a policy change required all full-time faculty to teach freshman comp, some who had not taught it for years came to those of us who have studied composition. It means developing a support group to increase awareness. It means raising our voices even when we have no vote. We spoke up at a departmental meeting and said we would rather have three or four full-time positions than five to eight part-time positions. This was enacted. Resistance meant, for me, refusing to accept an inferior contract with the English department and accepting one with the developmental department.

Though I am relatively new to the institution, many in similar positions have preceded me and have taken action. They raised their voices, and those in power heard and responded. Some have resisted by refusing to continue to teach. Though they loved teaching and were good at it, they had to take jobs in business for their emotional and financial survival. And the department has lost many excellent teachers. Some have stayed on and continue to resist in spite of frustrations and subtle censures. They advised me, "Get out of here. You will only be frustrated." But we are fortunate in having some full-time faculty who are sensitive to the position of the part-time teacher and take action also. They are the ones who send the inclusive memos, the ones who effect positive change. When such faculty become chairs of departments and committees, changes can take place.

On the other hand, my participation in such resistance must necessarily be tempered by my precarious and tenuous position. That position, in many institutions, is lower than that of the graduate student in status and lower than many of the university staff in salary and benefits. Constantly having everything to lose and no hope of gain, isolated nontenure-track teachers have tolerated the "intolerable" situations. Though our resistance at times may seem similar to that of sensitive "regular" faculty, it is practiced at greater risk. Unlike tenured faculty, the voices of those on term contracts can be easily silenced.

Am I naive to believe that my efforts and those of my peers will be heard rather than silenced? Will my efforts to resist help me or harm me? If I become more aware and more informed, will I be able to effect real change? I am both encouraged and discouraged. At times the hierarchy seems so entrenched that there seems little likelihood of change. At other times I feel hopeful. I have to believe our resistance can effect change. When I stop believing that, I will need to quit.

Will our growing number and the growing credibility of composition as a field of study give our collective voice the strength to be heard? Will that collective voice be joined by the voices of many "full-time" or "regular" faculty? Will the resisting voices of the Wyoming Conference

Resolution and similar voices within CCCC and NCTE and MLA who are petitioning and demanding attention to the issues concerning all nontenure track teachers be strong enough to be heard? Will the resulting dialogue move us from "call staff" status to "colleague" status?

July 10, 1989

I have chosen to return to graduate school and get my doctorate so that I can get a tenured position in order to help myself and my colleagues.

January 29, 1990

As I look over the text that has evolved here (is still evolving, in fact), I see that there can be no closure, no comforting summation. I have seen some exciting changes come about since I began. But I also bristled when the Fall '89 quarter began with introductions of our new "call staff." I felt somewhat defeated, but then perhaps the value of the term *call staff* is that it forces the oppressed to consider their oppression and to resist. Perhaps that very offensive term is better in that it doesn't hide the reality that other terms seem to. Our resistance must be to the realities of the situation, not just the terms.

I have come to see that resisting must be constant. We never arrive; I am learning to accept that and to feel a bit more comfortable with the discomfort of it. I continue to see the dangers of speaking out and the dangers of not speaking out.

Works Cited

Freire, Paulo. *Pedagogy of the Oppressed*. New York: Continuum, 1970.

Wallace, M. Elizabeth, ed. *Part-Time Academic Employment in the Humanities*. New York: Modern Language Association of America, 1984.

Singleton: Are we meaning by "resistance" taking a critical look at anything, everything? Is that what we mean? And [what about when] we come back to this question of "what is the university?" Is the purpose of, or any educational part along the way, is it to take critical looks at things? I hate that they say "critical thinking" as opposed to, you know, other thinking is uncritical—

Mack: Like creative writing.

Singleton: Thinking *means* doing it critically, so is resisting the same thing as taking a critical look at things? I don't know.

Reid: But if you teach people resistance, that's active. It sounds like all of our definitions of "resistance" have been active. That it's an action. Is that useful?

5

An Uncomfortable
State of Mind

Michael Blitz
C. Mark Hurlbert

We were back to definitions, back to finding a point — or points — from which to begin. Our terms, our "critical vocabularies," were fore-grounded in ways that some participants found disconcerting. How were we going to articulate courses of action if we were having so much difficulty understanding the language in which we write articles and books, teach students, present papers, and propose curricula? This is not to say that the language participants were using was obscure or particularly idiomatic. But we *were* discovering that even among a small group of educators specifically trying to work in common, it was proving difficult to *use* the current language of composition in common.

Teaching for critical consciousness, as a number of us agreed at the roundtables, causes, perhaps requires, an uncomfortable state of mind — for students *and* teachers. One source of the discomfort is in the attempts and failures of educators to acknowledge their own situation in the culture that we would encourage students and colleagues to resist. Our teaching, like the writing that we and our students do, is an elaboration of interests that our compositions generate, repeat, and/or maintain. As agents of an institution whose design is more and more visibly to uphold "characteristics of excellence" as defined by, for example, the Middle States Association, writing teachers committed to encouraging critical consciousness *and* action are in the potentially dangerous and endangering role of teaching people to challenge an institution's "mission." This is the kind of whistle-blowing that might very well bring about economic and social hardship among those who attempt it. In other words, the commitment involved in a critical

43

education extends far beyond a writing or literature pedagogy and entails very real risks in public life. But educators need to move beyond, as Nancy Mack pointed out in Seattle, becoming "cynical or ironic or, you know, melancholic, or whatever you do with depression from your critical consciousness." James Sledd wrote to the two of us that English teachers are not likely to "make a serious effort at serious resistance to the basic injustice of our social system as that system is embodied in our departments and professional organizations." It may be the case, as Sledd also said at the Chicago roundtable, "If you ask what the book [*Composition and Resistance*] can accomplish, I would say that we'd be crazy to expect it to accomplish a great deal. If there's to be real change in American education, there's got to be first real change in American society. And that will come only when enough people are miserable enough to say 'it will cost me less to fight than to resist.' So if we set out with any glorious ambitions, I think we're in for a terrible disappointment."

So what are the choices? None of us in this project could admit to being miserable in the ways that James Sledd implied. We are all employed, comfortably housed, and fed. For us, a melancholic critical consciousness may be hard academic currency. Besides, we hardly constitute a revolutionary front. Even if we perceived ourselves that way, we could not possibly agree on what the aims of a revolution should be. While American educators can, for example, celebrate events in Eastern Europe as examples of massive social revolutionary change, we ought to also note that some of the results of these trans-formations resemble the conservative capitalism and consumerism that social and economic critics blame for injustices and abuses in our own culture. The fact is we are teachers of English who work for academic "companies" that are increasingly in the service of bigger companies and organizations some of which actually encourage polite dissension. Nevertheless, such collective grumbling serves mainly to intensify ter-ritorial disputes within the academy as each group must ensure a new mob of educators "liberated" by the academy to be turned loose within it and companies like it and in support of it.

Isn't the profession empty if it can effect no social change other than the changing of the guard? What if the only reason to write and to read this book is to arm ourselves against the suspicion that the profession is an empty vessel? What would students do if teachers admittedly couldn't think of reasons to take composition except to enlist apprentice-writers in the keeping of the flame of the profession? Or, worse, in the refueling of the fires of a racist, sexist, classist, homophobic culture? If, for example, graduate students stopped reading books and articles on composition, teachers of *future* composition teachers would have to go home. One motive for studying composition as a discipline or for going to conferences, delivering papers, and having meetings is to demonstrate its academic integrity. Composition programs have to hold up under the scrutiny of accrediting associations, private funding agencies, university administrations, department heads and planners, and colleagues in literature.

Attempting to address the social relevance of teaching composition, participants proposed that we should teach students to recognize the general availability—or unavailability—of knowledge, and we ought to make our students uncomfortable with their socioeconomic status, but we couldn't agree toward what end. Some argued that, as English teachers, we are unlikely to do much of anything to challenge, let alone change, political and economic realities. Others suggested that even small-scale dialogues such as the ones we had been engaged in at the three roundtables are the beginning of significant social action. We discussed the fact that the business of educating has always been conducted primarily by women for men at the expense and abuse of women and that what we know, even about ourselves, are narratives that we can reread and reinterpret.

There's nothing like this in any of the descriptions of composition courses in our universities. Why, then, were we talking about these things? How are they the business of composition, the content of the discipline commonly considered to be in the "service" of "content courses"? Even as participants argued about "the discipline," we were, more and more, discovering our interests in making composition *uncertain* and *undisciplined*. A great many composition educators say that it is our obligation to teach students to write and read for and within curricula made by academics for academics. Others would say that our responsibility is to assist students in resisting these constraints. The former position is, for example, the traditional objective for con- servative writing across the curriculum programs. The latter view is, or perhaps has become, the definition of a critically (self-)conscious liberal education. Both views place students in the powerless position of having to resist abstractions rather than people and their actions and policies. But education could be something other than the programming of the new wave of consumers in and of culture. If education can do no more than this, maybe teachers should become counter-educators. Counter-educators can make what Donald Schön imagines as "a learning system conducive to the continual criticism and restructuring of organ- izational principles" (336). These principles would include the ways in which knowledge is organized and distributed, the ways in which students and teachers are managed, the ways in which educational institutions and corporate powers tend to each other's interests. Which is to say that the lives of teachers and students in all their contradictions, confusions, discomforts and comforts, and connections and disconnections to something typically called the "social whole" constitute the most pressing *subject*-matters.

Works Cited

Characteristics of Excellence in Higher Education: Standards for Accreditation. Commission on Higher Education of the Middle States Association of Colleges and Schools. 1982.

Schön, Donald A. *The Reflective Practitioner: How Professionals Think in Action.* New York: Basic, 1983.

6

Composition and Cultural Studies

James A. Berlin

A small group of us in the English department at Purdue have attempted a project in bringing together the methods of composition studies with the methods of cultural studies in a freshman writing course. The effort involves seven teaching assistants and fourteen course sections, each averaging twenty-three students. The course is one small response to the calls for a reconstituted English studies organized around the activity of cultural critique. Before describing its operation, it will be useful to examine the theoretical and historical grounds of the undertaking.

The methods and materials of composition studies in the modern university throughout its one-hundred-yerar history have anticipated many features of the recently formulated agenda of cultural studies. As I have tried to demonstrate in *Rhetoric and Reality: Writing Instruction in American Colleges, 1900–1985*, a number of the conspicuous paradigms appearing in the composition classroom during this time have taken as their province the critique of discursive practices in a broadly constituted cultural realm. Terry Eagleton has recently provided evidence, furthermore, that such an effort is entirely appropriate to the historical function rhetoric has performed in Western societies. Rhetoric has continually served as one of the central elements of education, providing the ruling orders the discursive weapons for managing economic, political, and cultural activities, focusing on the relations between language and power in order to secure dominant-group interests. The last point underscores the important difference in the versions of cultural studies now being forwarded: those of today are most likely to be presented in opposition to hegemonic social and political formations, rstifying strategies to locate the places of power and their rations. In the past, the university English department as operating in the transcendental realm of objective ing rhetorics that revealed the rightness of existing race, class, and gender relations. The cultural studies course described in this essay departs from this model both in its oppositional stance, critiquing rather than approving existing power relations, and in its admission of its own provisional and historical character.

Composition as cultural studies has received little attention in current discussions of English studies, a fact that gives it special force as an oppositional alternative. The reason for its silencing has to do with the invidious distinction between poetics and rhetoric that has characterized English departments since their beginning, a distinction that has valorized poetics while considering rhetorical texts and their production as not worth serious study.[1] Raymond Williams in *Marxism and Literature* offers the best explanation about the larger economic, political, and cultural developments that led to this situation. Gerald Graff in *Literature Against Itself* provides a clear discussion of the form this binary opposition has assumed in English studies. (Although he does not, I should add, use the term *rhetoric*, his discussion indicates the nature of the discourse that falls into this category from the point of view of current English department practices, as I have indicated in "Rhetoric, Poetics, and Culture: The Collapsing Boundaries of English Studies.") Graff outlines the distinction through a set of sharp oppositions: the narrowly representational rhetorical against the creative poetic; an epistemology of truth as correspondence against truth as creation; the bounded and constrained against the voyages into the unforeseen; the docile and habitual against the risky; texts as determinate objects against texts as indeterminate invitations for free play; and, finally, meaning as product against meaning as process. Given these contrasts, it is little wonder that rhetoric is relegated to the utility room of English studies. Graff offers these distinctions in order to deconstruct them in favor of poetics, arguing that both, when at their best, belong at the center of the poetic text. His operation is finally, then, as unfriendly to rhetoric as those he criticizes, reinscribing as it does the divisive oppositions he criticizes. Still, his analysis of current conditions is instructive. In *Textual Power*, Robert Scholes offers an account of the conflicting attitudes and practices in English departments that correspond to the distinctions Graff articulates: the devalorized production of the texts of rhetoric placed against the valorized consumption of literary texts; the simple, utilitarian and easily interpreted texts of the rhetorical against the complex and disinterested poetic; the lower-school study of reading and writing versus the university discipline of literary studies; and, finally, the commonplace and profane rhetorical against the sacred, priestly texts of the literary, in which beauty and truth are one.

This binary opposition between the sacred poetic and the profane rhetorical has been challenged on several fronts. Literary theorists from the left have questioned it, arguing that both kinds of texts are imbricated in economic, social, and political arrangements — are indeed ideological. In other words, they argue that both kinds of texts are products of culture and that both reproduce or resist culture in related ways. The poetics/rhetoric opposition has also been put under interrogation by deconstruction in its various forms, the position here being that all texts are the products of identical signifying practices, of discursivity, and that, in the end, all experience is text, all is linguistically constructed. Finally, rhetoric studies itself has resisted this binary opposition in the form of social constructionist and social-epistemic formulations. All of these studies destroy the invidious distinction between rhetoric and poetic, reconstituting it rather than reversing it, by arguing that both reward close examination since both share in the textuality of all experience; in other words, the two kinds of discourse are one in the complexity and reproductive capacity of their signifying practices, the differences having to do with culture itself — with ideologically inscribed values — not with any inherent and essential qualities. These three influences have converged in our shaping of the composition as cultural studies class at Purdue, most notably in our reliance on the speculation of members of the Birmingham Center for Cultural Studies.

In "What is Cultural Studies Anyway?" Richard Johnson, current head of the Birmingham Center, offers the definition of cultural studies we have followed: "cultural studies is about the historical forms of consciousness or subjectivity, or the subjective forms we live by, or, in a rather perilous compression, perhaps a reduction, the subjective side of social relations" (43). Johnson connects cultural studies to the post-structuralist project, arguing "that subjectivities are produced, not given, and are therefore the objects of inquiry, not the premises or starting-points" (49). Cultural studies is thus concerned with the ways social formations and practices are involved in the shaping of consciousness. Most important in subject formation, however, is the concern for the ideological, and here the Marxist dimensions of the Birmingham group become central. The relation between the social and the subjective is imbricated in economic, political, and cultural considerations that are always ideological and historically specific. Ideology, furthermore, is inscribed in language, in the signifying practices of social groups. These signifying practices are situated at the very center of cultural study since the subject is considered not as a transcendent and sovereign free agent but as an historical agent that is the point of intersection for ideologically inscribed discourses or cultural codes. The self is a social

t and the medium of construction is cultural discourse. Further-
......., ..J Stuart Hall, an early leader of the Birmingham group, points
out, a given language or discourse does not belong to any class, race,
or gender. Following Volosinov and Gramsci, he argues that language
is always an arena of struggle to make certain meanings—certain
ideological practices—prevail. Cultural codes thus are always in conflict,
are always competing for hegemony, for domination in defining consciousness. In other words, cultural codes compete in forwarding different agendas for the ways humans are to behave, and these are
always in conflict.

And now at last I am ready to turn to our experimental course.
Our intention is to locate the composing process within its social
context, combining the methods of semiotic analysis in considering
cultural codes with social-epistemic rhetoric. Thus, we are organizing
the course around an examination of the cultural codes, the social
semiotics, that are working themselves out in shaping consciousness in
our students. The focus is on the relation of current signifying practices
to the structuring of subjectivities—of race, class, and gender formations, for example—in our students and ourselves. Our effort is to
make students aware of the cultural codes—the various competing
discourses—that attempt to influence who they are . Our larger purpose
is to encourage our students to resist and to negotiate these codes—
these hegemonic discourses—in order to bring about more personally
humane and socially equitable economic and political arrangements.
We are thus strongly interested in locating the points at which students
are now resisting and negotiating, using these when they emerge as
points of departure for our dialogue. It is our hope that students who
can demystify the cultural codes they encounter will be motivated to
begin the reshaping of subjectivities and society. We are, in a sense,
engaging in a war of position rather than a war of maneuver, to use
Gramsci's formulation, hoping to encourage resisting, negotiating subjects within positions of power in the dominant culture. Our project
thus intersects with many in this collection, particularly those of Miriam
Chaplin, Jeff Golub and Louann Reid, Joseph Harris and Jay Rosen,
Kurt Spellmeyer, and Marian Yee.

This term we have undertaken six units: on the language of advertising, on work, on play, on education, on gender, and on the possibilities of individuality. The students read essays that articulate the
competing codes inscribed within the social formations that intersect
each of these topics. They then attempt to analyze the way these codes
have functioned in their own experience, paying particular attention to
the categories of gender, race, and class. For instance, after reading
and discussing Stuart Berg Flexner's "A Consumer's Guide to Social
Behavior," an essay about how advertising creates needs that can then

be satisfied for profit, Tom Wolfe's "Porno-Violence," and Alleen Pace Nilsen's "Sexism in English: A Feminist View" (all in Joseph Comprone's *Perspectives: Turning Reading into Writing*), students were asked to bring in a collection of magazine ads on a product of their choice. Their task was to apply what they had learned about cultural codes from this activity in evaluating the ways the advertisements were attempting to define and shape their behavior. The product of the unit was to be a 1,000-word essay to be written for an audience of their teacher and class peers concerning the effects of advertising on young people.

The major devices used to undertake this analysis were three simple but powerful semiotic strategies that function as heuristics. The first of these is the location of the binary oppositions inscribed in the texts—that is, the nature of the boundaries that give terms meaning. The second is the discovery of denotation and connotation as levels of meaning that involve contesting. The third is the reliance on invoking culturally specific narrative patterns—for example, the Horatio Alger myth or the Cinderella plot. These served as exploratory devices that enabled students to investigate semiotic codes as persuasive appeals, paying particular attention, once again, to the reliance of these codes on culturally specific categories of race, gender, and class. This inventional strategy was combined with a process approach to composing, with students engaging in free writing, creating multiple drafts, and participating in editorial groups and conferences with the teacher. Students also studied patterns of arrangement and stylistic strategies as the manifestation of similarly culturally coded activities.

The intention of forwarding this method is frankly political, an effort to prepare students for critical citizenship in a democracy, to teach them to "interrogate their texts," as Kurt Spellmeyer formulates it in another essay in this collection. We want students to begin to understand that language is never innocent, instead constituting a terrain of ideological battle. Language—textuality—is thus the scene where different conceptions of economic, social, and political conditions are contested with consequences for the formation of the subjects of history, the very consciousness of the historical agent. We are thus committed to teaching writing as an inescapably political act, the working out of contested cultural codes that affect every feature of our experience. This involves teachers in an effort to problematize students' experiences, requiring them to challenge the ideological codes they bring to college by placing their signifying practices against alternatives. Sometimes this is done in a cooperative effort with teachers and students agreeing about the conflicts that are apparent in considering a particular cultural formation—for example, the elitist and ruthlessly competitive organization of varsity sports in high schools. Students are able to locate points of personal resistance and negotiation in dealing with the injustices of this common social practice. At other times, the students and teachers are at odds with each other or, just as often, the students are themselves divided about the operation and effects of conflicting codes. This often results in heated exchange. The role of the teacher is to act as a mediator while insuring that no code, including her own, goes unchallenged.

As Stuart Hall has argued, in responding to the subject positions that texts create for their interpreters, the agent can submit, negotiate, or resist. The object of the course is to encourage in students, at the very least, a negotiation of the race, class, and gender codes they are commonly invited to accept in their encounters with school, work, and the media. To expect complete resistance is of course unrealistic. Teachers do, however, expect students to locate the discursive formations they have experienced, to thematize them in their writing, and in this way to locate any contradictions inscribed in them. Students who deny all contradiction—insisting that their experience has been one of peace, joy, and harmony—are continually challenged in this course (the results of which will be discussed shortly). Furthermore, our effort is to encourage in students both a critical response to their experience and a tolerance for the critical responses of others. Through this we hope they will become more questioning as citizens and more tolerant of diversity of opinion in the ongoing formation of a democratic society, a society committed to equity in its economic, social, and political arrangements.

The most remarkable effect of the course has been the intensity of resistance students have offered their teachers, a stiff unwillingness to problematize the ideological codes inscribed in their attitudes and behavior. This experience, it is somewhat consoling to report, we share with C. H. Knoblauch and Cecilia Rodríguez Milanés. Many students find it difficult—even painful—to offer any critique of the set of cultural codes they daily enact. For example, students have described advertisements as blatantly sexist, class-biased, and patently dishonest, and then gone on to praise them for their success in selling a product. Or writers have analyzed dishonest codes used in particular ads without commenting on their effectiveness or their ethics, attempting to avoid judgment in the name of scientific objectivity. Or students have described being exploited, harassed, and even abused on the job and, perhaps even more often, in a schoolroom, only to conclude that the experience was nonetheless valuable because it prepared them for the "real world." We finally had to discourage papers arguing that painful experiences were most often the best experiences "because they make you mature, independent, and self-reliant." (This strong inclination carried through into some students' final evaluations of the class: they praised it precisely because they disliked it so much.) In short, the attitude of a surprising number of students has been: Whatever is is right and incontestable. It is best to adjust. And it is good for you.

I am not rehearsing these experiences in order to engage in another round of school and student bashing. This generation of students has already become distinguished as one of the most harshly criticized and even vilified generations in recent memory. If the students of the sixties were labelled "the best and the brightest," these students have been characterized by leaders in government, business, and industry as "the worst and the most witless." Indeed, part of the unwillingness of our students to be critical of their experience can probably be attributed to a loss of confidence in themselves and their society, the continual questioning of their competence having taken its toll. These students are clearly victims of political strategies that have held their generation personally responsible for the failures of economic and social policies over which they have had no control. It is the schools, we are told, who are to blame for our nation's loss of competitiveness internationally, plant closings, lost jobs, and a reduced standard of living for a significant number of our citizens. The system is solid, but its young have become the weak link in the chain of economic growth and prosperity.

This course has been criticized by colleagues for indoctrinating students, on the one hand, and for failing to forward a political agenda, on the other. Often these contradictory objections have come from the same person. The issue is a complicated one. Against the charge of indoctrination we would say that we are not attempting to win mindless conformity from our students. They certainly do not have to take a leftist position on the issues they consider in their essays, and they rarely attempt to do so. As already indicated, most argue against a radical critique, preferring interpretations that are politically more conservative. We do insist, however, that students take into consideration the oppositional point of view continually forwarded by the teacher, by a number of the essays read, and by other students. In other words, students cannot ignore objections to the positions offered in their essays. Most students indeed find the leftist questioning of their cultural codes unconvincing, writing their essays counter to them — although there are numerous exceptions, particularly among women who begin to suspect the limits of culturally sanctioned gender codes. Students can thus disagree with the ideology forwarded by the teacher without fear of recrimination. Indeed, one of the more notable features of the course is that students do feel free to resist their teachers, to disagree rather than simply conform. The class thus encourages open debate and confrontation in students who have been prevented from protesting about any feature of their experience. Since most define themselves in contrast to what they see as the irresponsible rebelliousness of the sixties and seventies, this willingness to debate is salutary. In short, no indoctrination takes place.

The politics of the teachers in the course is, however, never concealed. The views offered by them are contestatory and socialist, supporting a radically democratic sharing of power in economic, social, political, and cultural areas. There is never any doubt in the minds of the students about where the teachers stand, and the teacher is always an important part of the audience for whom the student is writing. Thus, in preparing their essays and in serving as peer readers in editorial groups, students must assume a readership that includes both unsympathetic as well as sympathetic members, and this is true of the nascent socialists and feminists in the classroom as well as the devoted Reaganites. At the least, then, we are providing an environment that encourages tolerance and respect for diverse opinions, providing the opportunity for students to explore critically their own deepest convictions. The result, we hope, will be to encourage a more open and tolerant society, one in which the full possibilities of democracy might be openly explored.

One final word. Despite the resistance we have encountered, anonymous student evaluations of teachers in the program have fallen within the normal acceptable range for the freshman writing course. In fact, one of the teachers in our group won a department teaching award based on these evaluations, an unusual honor for a first-year teaching assistant. (This teacher, incidentally, experienced some of the strongest and most aggressive resistance of any of us.) I can also report that all teachers who participated are convinced that the program is worth continuing. Its inherent conflict provides a rich lesson for student and teacher in the rigor and promise of a dialogic rhetoric in a democracy.

Note

1. I have discussed this issue at length in "Rhetoric, Poetic, and Culture: Contested Boundaries in English Studies."

Works Cited

Berlin, James A. "Rhetoric, Poetic, and Culture: Contested Boundaries in English Studies." *The Politics of Writing Instruction*. Eds. Richard Bullock and John Trimbur. Portsmouth, NH: Boynton/Cook, 1991.

———. *Rhetoric and Reality: Writing Instruction in American Colleges, 1900–1985*. Carbondale: Southern Illinois UP, 1987.

Comprone, Joseph J. *Perspectives: Turning Reading into Writing*. Boston: Houghton Mifflin, 1987.

Eagleton, Terry. *Literary Theory: An Introduction*. Minneapolis: U of Minnesota P, 1983.

Graff, Gerald. *Literature Against Itself: Literary Ideas in Modern Society*. U of Chicago P, 1979.

Hall, Stuart. "Encoding/Decoding." *Culture, Media, Language*. Ed. Stuart Hall et al. London: Hutchinson, 1980.

——. "Recent Developments in Theories of Language and Ideology." *Culture, Media, Language*. Ed. Stuart Hall et al. London: Hutchinson, 1980.

Johnson, Richard. "What Is Cultural Studies Anyway?" *Social Text* 16 (1986–87): 38–80.

Scholes, Robert. *Textual Power: Literary Theory and the Teaching of English*. New Haven: Yale UP, 1985.

Williams, Raymond. *Marxism and Literature*. Oxford: Oxford UP, 1977.

Harris: I'm thinking about the relation of our students to the mass media, and I think this addresses some of your concerns, Nancy, that mass media be seen as more than simply perniciously manipulative. I mean my students are creatures of the mass media. So am I, in certain ways. And there's a tremendous amount of pleasure and meaning and insight and joy to be found in those images. And there's, to a certain degree—I mean, we have to be willing to admit to that. My first instinct was to take essentially a more or less critical and aggressive stance toward [media images] almost entirely. And pretty soon students, as Jim [Berlin] has reported, begin to feel like they're the ones being criticized. And it seems to me, I mean this is not a panacea, but what I've been doing in the last few years is to try to identify some common ground, you know, some of the music, the shows, the films, the ads that we *like*, and that we would endorse and the part of that good life that we think, "Yeah, that's us, too," and then to sort of fall back and say—

Golub: Yeah, but see, the difference between you and your students is that you have a choice. You could look at something, you can say, "I like this part, I don't like this part, I see what they're doing here, I don't"—the students don't have that choice. They're the victim—

Berlin: What? About media, you mean? About—

Golub: Yeahhhh—

Berlin: Why don't they have the choice? I mean, why can't we give them the choice and say—Well, they think they have the choice anyhow.

Golub: We give them the choice by making them aware of the how the stuff is done and—

Berlin: Yeah—

Golub: And so once you show, for instance, junk mail, then you can say, "Do you still want to buy this thing?" And some students say, "Yes." At least now they have a choice.

Berlin: Yeah. Well I agree. But I don't understand how you—it seems to me the same point he's [Harris] making over here—

Golub: Alright, well, I just mentioned that it was more like you said what worked for you was to use the media, I seized on that. But the difference is that I think our critical thinking is developed to a much higher degree than the students'—

Berlin: Oh, sure—

Golub: And that's a crucial difference—I mean—

Berlin: Right, but that's what we're trying to equalize, though, right? I mean we try to, that's resistance. Back to "resistance," right? We try to resist the designs on them. I don't think anybody here would disagree that those designs are often not in the best interests of the students, or that the designs on us are not in our own best interests or in the interests of somebody who's going to make a buck on us—

Knoblauch: In fact it's interesting. The crusading teacher is also a media image.

Mack: Mmmhmm—

Berlin: Yeah—

Hurlbert: Right!

Knoblauch: Witness *Dead Poets Society*, where, by the end, you've got one dead student and a teacher who stood up on a desk, big deal. (laughs)

Berlin: Right.

Knoblauch: I mean, what're they trying to sell in a movie like that? That teachers, you know, buy stuff like that—

7

Teaching Writing as Cultural Criticism

Joseph Harris
Jay Rosen

We would like our title to be read in two ways. Our first concern is with how to teach students to write as critics of their culture, to reflect on those discourses—of the home, school, church, media, work, neighborhood, and so on—of which they are part. But we also want to talk about teaching itself as a form of cultural criticism, about classrooms that do not simply reproduce the values of our universities and cultures but that also work to resist and question them.

In talking about teaching writing as cultural criticism, then, we mean to identify not only a subject but a stance. We want to form a view of our work as teachers that involves something more than simply helping students write "better"—at least so long as "better" only means more able to meet the demands put on them by one institution or the other, to write better themes, better reports, better memos, better term papers, and the like. And we want to talk about that work in terms other than those of "initiating" students into "academic discourse." Not that we imagine some sort of free space to which students can be guided—a space where they can write as they want to, unconstrained by the rules and demands of discourses and institutions. Quite the opposite. A writer is always situated, always constrained. But she can work not only within but *against* the limits of a discourse to find a position she can claim as her own. And that is what we want our students to do.

Let us begin by making some distinctions between the concepts of *discourse* and *community* that we think useful in working toward a more critical practice as teachers and intellectuals. We are troubled by the ways many recent theorists have imagined what a "discourse community" might be and how it might function. It is now commonplace to argue that one masters a discourse through entering into the community that uses it, by accepting the practices and values of that community as one's own. The concepts of discourse and community are linked together so often that the two almost seem interchangeable (as when "learning academic discourse" gets rephrased as "entering the academic community"). This conjoining blurs useful differences between the two terms. *Community* ceases to describe a local and specific group, and we are left instead with a vague and sentimental notion of individuals sharing a "collective project." Similarly, the idea of *a* "community of discourse" works to hide the fact that many communities include not one but several competing discourses — and that many discourses are more disruptive or isolating than they are binding in their effects. (This is particularly true of the discourses of the mass media, about which we will have more to say later.) Instead, discourse seems more often pictured as something that the members of a community own and control. This in turn leads to a transmission metaphor for learning in which experts initiate novices into the beliefs and practices of the community. In acquiring a new discourse the student is seen as moving from one community to another, as leaving behind old ways of interpreting in order to take on new forms of organizing experience. Learning is thus equated with assimilation, acculturation, conversion. As Patricia Bizzell has put it: "Upon entering the academic community, [students are] asked to learn a new dialect and new discourse conventions, but the outcome of such learning is acquisition of a whole new world view" (297).

Such views of community fail to suggest how a writer might form an oppositional or critical stance toward a discourse. Rather, she is seen as either working *inside* the constraints of a certain community or as remaining *outside* its projects and concerns — and to be outside is to be nowhere at all, with no real chance of being heard. The metaphor is spatial. It pictures various communities of discourse as having, in effect, different rooms of their own, and represses the idea that a writer can be part of several competing discourses at once.

We want to argue for a view of discourse that is not bound to such sovereign and utopian imaginings of community. A *discourse*, as we are using the term, is something like what Bakhtin called a "speech genre," an inherited set of rules and constraints for using language. The various disciplines and professions have their own discourses, which they attempt to police and refine, but they and the culture at large are also interpellated by broader discourses of gender, class, religion, individualism, ethnicity, and so on. David Bartholomae has argued that we find ourselves always already working within the constraints of such discourses. That is, we do not so much decide to appropriate them as discover that they have appropriated us; their constraints are imposed rather than chosen. This is as true when one writer accepts a certain discourse as her own (the teacher who sits down to write something called "literary criticism" or "composition theory") as it is when another resists its claims (the student who turns in a joycean narrative in the place of a term paper). The writer may accept or flaunt the conventions of her discourse; she may even try to transform them. But she cannot choose what they will be. Rather, they are always already in place, are the very conditions which make her writing possible.

But while groups and individuals alike attempt to use and control discourse for their own ends, neither can do so fully. Communities have borders; discourses do not. Rather, they spill over from one community to another — so that a single discourse may prove a shaping force in the thought and writing of several communities, and a single community turn out to be the site of many discourses. Psychoanalysis offers an apt example of how a discourse can elude the attempts of a community to define and control it. Despite the repeated attempts of Freud to define its proper aims and methods, the ways of thinking suggested by analysis soon grew beyond not only his control but beyond that of the psychiatric profession as well, becoming one of the most pervasive influences — though one that in many cases Freud would have reproved — on the culture at large. The peculiar history of rock and roll offers another instance. Here was a music that began by defining itself against the mainstream culture of its day and then within two decades became the mainstream culture, or at least one of the most salient parts of it — a co-opting which has led to the ironic re-appropriating of pop rock by various artists (UB40 sings Sonny and Cher) and audiences (the camp revival of The Monkees). And in the case of the mass media, we confront an entire machinery for distributing discourses *across* communities. That, after all, is the very principle employed by a television network — to create a "national" audience by delivering a certain kind of discourse, usually given the name "enter-tainment," to every community in the land.

Certainly there are specialized and technical discourses whose practices are confined to select groups of persons and whose influence does not extend much beyond them. But to take such communities (Masons, particle physicists, lepidopterists) as models of how discourse works seems misleading. A look at other sorts of groups (English departments, city neighborhoods, labor unions, writing classrooms) often shows the workings not of consensus but difference. Everyday experience suggests that more often than not we find ourselves working, studying, or living with people who act and think in ways quite unlike our own. And so while recent theory posits sets of beliefs and practices shared by entire disciplines and schools of thought, we often find few signs of this consensus in the talk and work that goes on in departments, classrooms, conferences, and the like.

If the aims of our teaching were professional in the narrowest sense — if our goals were simply to teach students how to do a certain well-defined form of literary criticism (or of economics or anthropology or chemistry) — then such metaphors of consensus and initiation might hold some limited use for our work. (Though even then to talk of a discourse as if it could be bracketed away from other modes of inter-preting, practiced in some sort of pure form, seems suspect. Recall Chomsky's remark that he first went to study with Zelig Harris because he liked his politics.) But if our aims are not so narrow, then we need to ground our teaching in a view of discourse that centers not on consensus but on difference and change. Mary Louise Pratt offers the beginnings of such a view in a recent essay that criticizes what she calls the "linguistic utopias" of theory and argues instead for a study of "the workings of language across rather than within lines of social differen-tiation, of class, race, gender, age" (61). Rather than theorizing about the workings of separate and autonomous "interpretive communities," Pratt suggests that we examine those "zones of contact" — schools, churches, workplaces, public meetings, and the like — in which various discourses meet and conflict.

One such "zone of contact" that comes to mind is, of course, the writing classroom — a space in which the differences between our own discourses, those of the university, and those of our students often become strikingly clear. By viewing the classroom as such a zone — as a site where different discourses are contested rather than as some sort of entry point into an imagined "community of academic discourse" — we can begin to see our work as an ongoing criticism of discourses both within and outside our universities. Min-zhan Lu has argued that what students need to do in learning the languages of the university is not to leave one community in order to enter another but to *reposition* themselves in relation to several continuous and conflicting discourses. By dramatizing these conflicts, the writing class can create a set of chances for such repositioning — or criticism — to occur.

So it turns out to be through setting up a kind of community — a zone of contact — that we can begin to question the power of discourse. Not only are the two concepts no longer interchangeable, they are in ways opposed. Nowhere is this more strikingly shown than in a class that takes the discourses of the mass media as its focus. For by having students talk together about the sorts of texts they are used to consuming in private, such a class can reconvene a small section of the scattered audiences of radio, film, and TV as a face-to-face group — thus making the discourses of those media available for criticism in ways they usually are not.

A scene from Sidney Lurnet's 1976 movie *Network* will help make this point clear. Early in the movie, Howard Beale, an aging TV newsman who has gone a bit crazy, urges his viewers to rise from their chairs, open the windows, and shout out: "I'm mad as hell, and I'm not going to take it anymore!" As one viewer after another follows Beale's instructions, we witness an extraordinary social transformation. The television audience begins to disintegrate and, as neighbors go to their windows to listen for one another's shouts, a kind of crude community of the angry and dispossessed is formed in its place. In turning toward one another, Beale's viewers immediately shift their status. They are no longer spectators separately attending to television, and because of this they can no longer be sold to advertisers as a commodity. Beale has thus used television to dismantle the "product" of the television industry, which is not only an audience, but an audience arranged in a certain way — as individual viewers, physically scattered and typically silent as they attend to the images on the screen.

Writing teachers can undertake a similar act by encouraging students to turn toward one another in order to examine and discuss the mass media in the various forms of television, radio, advertising, popular music, film, and fashion. Students come to the university with long experience as part of the audiences for these media. If they share a common culture, it is that of the sitcom, the pop song, and the thirty-second spot. If they have mastered any canon of great works, it is one that includes *The Honeymooners*, *Saturday Night Fever*, and Michael Jackson's *Thriller*. And if there is a culture that we, as their teachers, share with them it is much more likely to come from the mass media than from history, literature, or art. Attending in class to this common culture can thus offer us a chance not only to urge students towards a more conscious and critical stance towards the media but also to suggest the sorts of power and insight that the discourses of the university can offer them.

John Dewey remarked in *Democracy and Education* that: "There is more than a verbal tie between the words common, community and communication. Men live in a community in virtue of the things they have in common; and communication is the way they come to possess things in common" (4). While such a statement may seem nearly self-evident, we believe that television and the other mass media have in a sense proved Dewey wrong. For one of the most striking aspects of our current culture is the presence of a kind of *communication without community* — a continuous hail of information whose sources are usually vague ("Madison Avenue" or "the networks"), that is typically received by its viewers or listeners in the isolation of their living rooms, cars, or walkmen, and whose content is rarely discussed among them. ("What did you do last night?" "Nothing, just watched TV.")

Any stand-up comedian knows that the language of television advertising is hilarious when repeated on stage. "I'm not a doctor, but I play one on TV." No exaggeration or comic twist is required; the laughs come instantly the moment the language is recognized. We laugh because for the moment we are relieved to be free of the absurd demands that TV regularly makes upon us — to treat the impossible claim as plausible and the ridiculous pretense as serious, to respond to the TV doctor as if he actually *were* a doctor when he goes on to recommend a particular brand of cough medicine. The comedian allows us to share our experience of the ad as absurd. Our common awareness of the extremity of the claims made by the ad overpowers its ability to persuade, to be taken seriously.

It is precisely this sort of bond of common knowledge and experience that TV works to deny its viewers. Another way of putting it is to say that television tends to preempt common sense — that sort of understanding of the world that depends on and springs from the everyday interchanges that take place among the members of a social group. This preempting of a *common* sense is possible, first, because the TV audience is usually scattered, silent, and inert, and, second, because we have grown used to treating everything on TV as inconsequential, not worth discussing, a passing parade of images that goes on and on no matter what we think about it or how we respond to it.

We are not claiming that TV watchers are helpless blobs whose passive wants and desires are ceaselessly re-formed by every huckster on the box. But we are arguing that, in a variety of ways, TV encourages a kind of listlessness, a dullness of mind and spirit that is often experienced as boredom but that also has much to do with the anxiety and even loneliness of the solitary viewer. The writing classroom can reverse these conditions, bringing students together face-to-face as speakers and listeners who can verify, validate, and, in some cases, contest one another's reactions to TV. A good many of these reactions, of course, will be enthusiastic — and rightfully so. On TV there are any number of well-drawn characters, compelling stories, truly funny comics, and effective parodies. There is occasionally good writing on television, and often a great deal of stunning imagery. In short, there is pleasure and meaning to be found all over the dial, and a teacher who is unable to see this and convey some of her own enthusiasm for TV will not get very far with most students. But almost no one, teacher or student, can react with as much enthusiasm for television as television has for itself. Almost no one behaves as television wishes us to behave.

To suggest some of the ways in which this is true, we have at times brought into our classes a tape of a sitcom with a laugh track. What we have found is that many of the jokes that win laughs on the laugh track are so crude or inept that students react with either an uneasy silence or expressions of shared disdain. That in itself is not surprising, given the quality of writing and acting in a typical TV comedy. But there is more going on here than that. As the laughs issue from the TV set, a gulf begins to open between the writing class as a social group and the imaginary audience that the show is trying to assert. Students identify with the reactions of their classmates more than with those of the simulated audience — in part because they can see and hear each other and are thus accountable for their responses in ways they usually are not. And so they withdraw from membership in TV's imagined community of hearty laughers and instead begin to see themselves in the new role (for which they are well qualified) of media critics.

This refusal of twenty or so students to laugh along with a laugh track is quite different from the silence of a single viewer watching at home — different because the social setting of the classroom gives power and meaning to the students' collective rejection of the TV discourse. The strategy of the laugh track is to suggest to the isolated viewer that others are laughing, even if she is not. But when the others posited by the TV discourse are present in the classroom, watching the sitcom together in a space reserved for the common study of texts, the responses of the group become proof of the laugh track's manipulativeness.

We might seem to be making too much of this encounter with the laugh track, which may, after all, suggest nothing more than the desire of students to feel superior to the laughing audience simulated by TV. But that is precisely the point. Convened as a small group of speakers and listeners, the students *are* superior to the implied audience of the TV sitcom — since the classroom provides them with a zone of contact, a space in which their responses to TV can be shared and contested. At home, a viewer is offered only the choice of laughter or silence — both equally lacking in meaning when they take place in isolation. But in the classroom, silence becomes almost unbearable; television suddenly seems to demand comment — since to be silent is to risk communicating to the others in the class that, in fact, one *is* the sort of passive and accepting viewer implied by the TV show. To speak up about television is to defend oneself against the ways in which TV attempts to position its subjects — as scattered and isolated viewers who have lost the resources of common sense. When students begin to defend themselves in class this way, they move away from a private and toward a public sphere — which is precisely what Howard Beale was urging his viewers to do: to create out of their isolated feelings of anger, boredom, and helplessness the beginnings of a common world.

Mass communication, as we see it, is communication in the absence of such a "common world" — in which the members of an audience receive the same messages but do not have the chance to share,

interpret, and dispute them with one another. (Viewed this w
university lecture classes can be seen as a kind of mass commu......_,
since generally such courses act to transmit information without offering
students much chance to discuss it among themselves.) What makes
something a "mass medium," then, is not some set of physical properties
(as the debates about "electronic" versus "print cultures" would suggest)
but the *typical circumstances in which its messages are sent and interpreted*. For instance, even though they operate on the same physical
principles as commercial radio, walkie-talkies and CBs do *not* usually
function as mass media — since their typical uses easily allow listeners
and speakers to trade places. Similarly, what separates works of
"literature" from popular fiction are not differences in their uses of
language so much as the varying ways and circumstances in which they
are usually read, as we can see each time a bestseller from the past —
Great Expectations, Uncle Tom's Cabin, Dracula — is transformed into
a work for classroom study.

If literature, then, is whatever gets taught, mass culture is what
doesn't. Our point is that we can help students change the stances they
take toward the media by altering the circumstances in which they
interpret its discourses — by bringing TV out of the living room and
into the classroom. An anecdote will help suggest why we see this as a
useful goal for a class in writing.

In many of the classes we teach, we ask students to bring in an
advertisement from a magazine that particularly interests them. The
most popular choices are always cigarette and cosmetic ads. When we
ask students to read the strategies behind the ads they have selected,
they usually say something like: "Well, they're trying to say that if you
smoke Marlboros then you'll become as macho as this guy here." We
then ask: "Is that what *you* think when you look at the ad? Do *you*
really figure that just by smoking Marlboros you can become the
Marlboro man?" Of course not, they reply, they're not fooled by this
obvious ploy — *but other people are*. We find this response interesting —
since these "other people" are almost never known personally to the
students who cite them as the victims of advertising. They're not
friends, family members, or the other students in the class. So who are
they? One day a student gave a compelling answer. Who are these
people who fall prey to the claims of advertising? "The masses," he
said. Who are the masses? "The people who this ad is aimed at," he
replied.

We think that this student was right, that he had, perhaps without
fully knowing it, uttered much more than a simple tautology. Raymond
Williams once argued: "There are no masses; there are only ways of
seeing people as masses" (289). The term refers not to a particular
group or class of people but to people addressed in a certain way. "The

masses," in other words, are a way of imagining the audience. And so the laugh track on TV is a way of getting us to imagine ourselves as members of a mass of viewers, much as the seductions of advertising picture us as part of a mass of consumers whose wants and desires are aroused and sated by its parade of items and images. To the degree that we acquiesce to the roles the media imagines for us, we are all part of "the masses."

And so the student who spoke of the masses as the victims of advertising was actually naming the implied reader of the Marlboro ad. But it's uncertain how aware he was of the odd status of this reader — never a specific individual, yet at one moment or the other all of us. One job of the writing class, then, might be to try to reveal this curious position that mass culture places us all in, to suggest both the sorts of claims the media make upon us and the possibilities of resisting them. The writing class can do this because it brings students face-to-face with others like themselves who do not always behave as the media want them to. This does not mean, of course, that those who "see through" the tactics of the mass media are somehow immune from their influence. But it does allow us to talk about those influences in more complex and useful ways. Rather than positing some other class of people whose desires are wholly under the sway of advertising, students can be pushed to look at their own conflicting desires — some of which are reflected with uncanny accuracy in the ads. And in looking at the ways the media position them as masses, they may also begin to see that they are more than that too — that they are smarter than the implied audience of much of the media, that they deserve better.

We have tried to show here how setting up the classroom as a zone of contact can help students grow more aware of, and perhaps even resist, some of the ways in which they are positioned by the media. We don't mean to suggest, though, that such a class can give students a set of critical skills that they can then apply with equal results to all situations and discourses. For the gains of criticism are always local and strategic. They do not coalesce into the workings of some sort of "critical discourse" — some set of fixed moves and practices that give one power over language. It is often noted that the hardest position to criticize is your own. This would not be true if such a set of skills and practices existed to be drawn upon.

Instead, criticism is often the result of serendipity and desire: on the chance meetings of discourses, persons, and texts — and on the inclination of a writer to look for and pursue the differences such meetings reveal. We are sometimes placed in ways that let us see certain texts or events in a different or unusual light — and it is at those points that we can begin to resist the power of discourses, to transform their rules, to become critics. As teachers of writing, our task is to arrange such meetings in our classrooms, which are, after all, not only zones of contact but also spaces of possibility.

Note

The beginning drafts of this piece were first presented at a panel on Teaching Writing as Cultural Criticism at the 1989 CCCC in Seattle. We owe thanks to our friend and colleague on that panel, Robert von der Osten, for his help in conceiving this project, as well as to Stephen Carr, Bruce Horner, and Min-zhan Lu for their useful readings of our work.

Works Cited

Bakhtin, M. M. "The Problem of Speech Genres." In *Speech Genres and Other Late Essays*. Trans. Vern W. McGee. Ed. Caryl Emerson and Michael Holquist. Austin: U of Texas P, 1986.

Bartholomae, David. "Inventing the University." *When a Writer Can't Write: Studies in Writer's Block and Other Composing-Process Problems*. Ed. Mike Rose. New York: Guilford, 1985.

Bizzell, Patricia. "What Happens When Basic Writers Come to College?" *College Composition and Communication* 37 (1986): 294–301.

Dewey, John. *Democracy and Education*. New York: Macmillan, 1966.

Lu, Min-zhan. "Writing as Repositioning." *Journal of Education* 172 (1990): 18–21.

Pratt, Mary Louise. "Linguistic Utopias." *The Linguistics of Writing: Arguments between Language and Literature*. Ed. Nigel Fabb, Dereck Attridge, Alan Durant and Colin MacCabe. New York: Methuen, 1988.

Williams, Raymond. *Culture and Society*. New York: Columbia UP, 1983.

Singleton: I got to thinking about the evaluations that my students give, and part of my trying to get them to write honestly, "Tell me what you really think, should I do this in the future," and giving them this openness, this power to speak out and say what they think. One of the ways they're using it is on these evaluations of me and some of the other teachers. And that's one place where they feel like they could speak out, and so they are speaking out, they are taking that empowerment, not given to them, but that they have grasped hold of, and are using it to say, "I didn't like this." I think it's [a] wonderful discomfort that we're causing them because they're having to take responsibility for their own education.

Reid: I think I'm a little bothered, in the devil's advocate sort of mode, by the idea that causing discomfort is a worthwhile goal.

Singleton: Ooooh, did somebody say it was a worthwhile goal?

Reid: No, I, I'm saying—

Singleton: I think it's something that happens sometimes, but I don't know if that's—

Mack: On the way to a worthwhile cause—

Singleton: —the intention—

Knoblauch: *I'll* say it's a worthwhile goal just for the sake of argument! [laughter]

Reid: No, no, I really didn't mean it to come off as what you said. I meant it as sort of an overall feeling that I am absorbing that we can't let them be complacent, and certainly I'm not in favor of complacency, but it sounds like, well, so we need to stir them up, we need to make them uncomfortable. And I don't know whether it's, maybe it's, I don't know, it seems like the other side of that is that we also need to help them. I mean, I have fifteen-, sixteen-, seventeen-, eighteen-year-olds who need to understand what they can do to get along with society, and I don't want to say to fit in with society, but certainly that's a worthwhile teenage goal.

Berlin: Yeah—

Singleton: I don't think we have to teach them *that*. I mean they are really determined to fit in—

Reid: But I don't think—

Singleton: I mean their clothes, their language, their cars—

Reid: But I don't think, well, I mean, I don't know. I—

Singleton: But you mean with the adult society.

Reid: Yeah.

Singleton: Well, I don't know, if they're ready to or if they need to. They'll do that when they have to. That's part of youth—

Berlin: Oh, but—

Reid: But I mean, but isn't helping them to learn and grow and mature helping them to understand what society is?

Singleton: But don't they know when they hit up against it and it doesn't work?

Berlin: Yeah.

Singleton: I don't know that we have to teach them that, do we?

Reid: I don't know. I don't know if you can, I don't want to say protest against it, but I can't think of another word at this hour, but I'm not sure that you can help them to "resist," whatever that is, unless they understand it.

8

Knowledge Against "Knowledge"
Freshman English, Public Discourse, and the Social Imagination

Kurt Spellmeyer

Theory

In his ethnography of undergraduate life at Rutgers, *Coming of Age in New Jersey*, the anthropologist Michael Moffatt offers the following observation:

> American college professors officially renounced their own interest in the "whole student" ... almost a century ago, [after] they professionalized as academic specialists. To be a professional is to be interested in a narrow segment of expert knowledge; and, to ever-increasing degrees, this is what most American college professors are in the late twentieth century. And this is also what most college students are trying to become.[1]

When he maintains that we can no longer even imagine the academy as anything other than a loose federation of specialties, Moffatt identifies a change in the character of knowledge, a change after which the teaching of "composition" has become somewhat less credible. Faced with an unparalleled diversity of languages, both across and within the disciplines, we have been obliged to re-examine an article of faith our predecessors seldom questioned — their belief in the persistence of a genuinely public discourse, sustained by a tradition reaching back, as one Yale professor of English could still hold at the close of World War II, to "the Greeks and the Hebrews."[2] Without a particle of irony or wishful thinking, this same professor, Henry Seidel Canby, announced in his widely used freshman textbook that "Exposition is the most practical of all forms of writing. The power of clear expression is something required by every man in every walk of life."[3]

But "life," as I say, has been changed by a progressive specialization of learning inside the academy, one consequence of the ever greater division of labor beyond it. We have come to suspect that belletristic themes of the kind once composed for Canby at Yale will do little to prepare students now for their assignments on adolescent development, normative orientations, or world systems theory. Fifteen years of increasing confusion and debate have shown, if they show anything at all, how irrevocably "higher learning" has abandoned the larger project that created English 101. A few of us have elected to retool by teaching students to write as psychologists write, or sociologists, or political scientists. Others, the less epistemologically ambitious, have reduced their concerns to thesis, organization, and subject-verb agreement. Still others have attempted to counter the fragmentation of Language into languages by pursuing through cognitive science a unity absent within the curriculum. The dilemma of college English has been complicated further by the discovery that knowledge itself, which formerly seemed so benign and accessible, is irreparably "contaminated," and in fact always was, by interests arising from class, race, gender, logocentrism, logophobia, reification, mystification, ideology, and power.

At no risk of hyperbole we could say that the ground has dropped out from underneath us. And yet whatever liabilities our current, groundless situation entails, I would like to propose that it makes possible a uniquely immediate understanding of the relationship between higher learning and social life as a whole — a social life whose wholeness, real or potential, has grown increasingly hard to discern. Whereas the psychologist, the sociologist, and the political scientist might still be able to view their respective disciplines as a coherent explanation of "things as they really are," no teacher of writing can presuppose the centrality of his field, or of any field at all. Standing halfway in and halfway out of the language-games we play, many of us have had to reinvent a lingua franca on the spot, fashioned from the materials lying closest to hand. If this haphazard and uncircumspect activity might be mistaken for a sign of our professional desperation, it can also be seen as something closer to determined resistance. Tacking from discipline to discipline, crossing over from outside to inside and back, we have reaffirmed, more or less unknowingly, the possibility of public discourse in a shared social world — though not, with due respect to Henry Seidel

Canby, as an unchanging legacy of the past, but as a utopian ideal implicit in our present extemporaneous practices.

Institutionally liminal, we share with our students a perspective forgotten by the specialists who have mistaken their paradigms for a totality. Like us, these students occupy a fragmented "multiverse" of discourse, coherent only through their own countervailing efforts at reintegration. Another observer of the undergraduate scene, Jürgen Habermas, conjectured twenty years ago that a sense of coherence — which he defined as the awareness of a "singular parallel" between the private and the political — survives only among students from the so-called developing world, where technology has yet to rebuild higher learning in its own all-consuming image. After a century of such rebuilding, universities throughout the industrial West are rapidly contracting the scope of their activities to the production and trans-mission of "technically exploitable knowledge."[4] But it could also be argued, as a footnote to Habermas, that the United States represents a special instance of this phenomenon, since our distrust of history, our uneasiness with the pre-bourgeois, pre-technological legacy of Europe, has made the contraction of higher learning more thorough here than anywhere else. Ironically, by rejecting an elitist, backward-looking curriculum on behalf of economic "realities" and the "common man," the Progressive Era reform of higher education in America actually *widened* the distance between the classroom and the social life-world beyond it. Writing at the height of the reform, John Dewey warned against our failure to distinguish between a curriculum that simply "trained" students for the narrowly circumscribed activities of the workplace and one that promoted deliberation about the terms and direction of these activities.[5] By neglecting such deliberation, the "rationalization" of knowledge would foster, he insisted, a more per-vasive irrationality, compelling students to learn without permitting them to understand — to overcome the discontinuities between "knowl-edge" and the world they know.

Even after Dewey's contemporaries had begun to believe him, little could really be done. One late-Progressive Era work that attempted to resist the dis-sociation of higher learning was Jay William Hudson's *The College and New America*, published in 1920. Although Hudson, a professor of philosophy at the University of Missouri, recognized the need for increasing specialization, he was also convinced that the whole of social life could not be reduced to its academic parts, even those parts — the new social sciences — designed to comprehend the whole. "Presumably," he wrote, the social sciences are "about a very concrete thing called Society. But where and when does the student learn of that living Society, of which each social science represents only one limited aspect?"[6] To this metadisciplinary, almost metaphysical, question, none of the disciplines could furnish any answer. Nor could Hudson himself, except to call rather vaguely for an undergraduate curriculum that would inspire "the feeling and the conviction of responsibility to the social order, including its political institution."[7] Hudson and his like-minded contemporaries had no desire to resurrect the academic old guard, but they feared that the pragmatic reorganization of knowledge was already eroding the "mighty thing called public opinion," the public discourse through which established practices and values could be assessed, reformed, and reproduced.[8]

In a sense, Moffatt's ethnography attempts to answer, or at least renew, the question posed by Hudson, although he phrases it somewhat differently. Moffatt might say that Hudson underestimated the capacity of students to supply the missing social dimension of knowledge—to reintegrate the "local" experience of lectures and labs into larger structures of cultural meaning. The students Moffatt interviewed typically regarded "academics" as one part of the larger formative experience they called "college life." It seems to me this example, and much else in *Coming of Age*, overturns the image of undergraduates as the powerless subjects of our cultural engineering, an image that greatly exaggerates the degree of engineering we are able to bring off. At the same time, however, his work suggests the limits of their powers of reintegration. He notes, for example, the growing "privatization" of the campus and the decline of extracurricular organizations. According to Moffatt, "The students' general preference for private pleasures over group involvements" was "related to tendencies in the larger culture, to the shape of American individualism in the late twentieth-century."[9] While these students manage to preserve some connection between learning and "life," they appear to do so by excluding, to various degrees in various contexts, the social character of both.

Moffatt's research considered in toto suggests that Hudson's fears were not unjustified. Granting that few undergraduates leave Rutgers as Weberian "specialists without spirit, sensualists without heart," we have many good reasons for concluding, nevertheless, that the university fails to promote a social imagination, an awareness of the human "world" as a common historical *project*, and not simply a state of nature to which we must adjust ourselves. Nowhere was this absence of a social imagination more obvious to Moffatt than in the attitude of white students toward their black counterparts, whose distinctive patterns of behavior the whites characteristically misread as "unfriendliness," an intentional deviation from the "normal" code of sociability. "Given the students' pervasive individualism," he concludes, "no adequate alternative explanation" was "readily available to them." So fully did white students presuppose an individual—as opposed to social—basis for human behavior that they attributed all departures from the "normal" code to

cter. As Moffatt puts it, "you were unworthy of friendship
very essence: you were a 'phony,' an 'asshole,' a 'wimp,'
faggot.'"[10] Although his subjects saw "college life" and
_____ as complementary aspects of their educational experience,
the second did not usually make the first problematic, did not induce
students to devise alternative explanations for day-to-day events.

When their field of cultural vision has contracted so sharply that
"social life" is now a synonym for things they would never try to do in
mixed company, these "privatized" undergraduates can scarcely be
expected to notice the contradiction between yesterday's lecture on the
function of free choice in a market economy and the homeless people
they see sleeping on the floor at Penn Station when they go to New York
for the weekend. (Of course, a similar criticism might be lodged, with far
greater justice, against us, the specialists our students are trying to
emulate.) I find it encouraging, all the same, that the undergraduates in
Moffatt's study who became intellectually active — who entered into a
conversation with, and against, the academy — somehow developed an
attentiveness to the discontinuities between "knowledge" and knowledge. One of his subjects, for instance, a student called Lisa, was
gradually transformed during her years at Rutgers from an "all-American
cheerleader," by her own account, into someone who had learned to
"fight for my rights — specifically, my right to be intelligent." For me, the
most telling aspect of Lisa's evolution as a thinker is the critical stance she
adopts toward "truth" itself. "I tend to question," she told Moffatt,
"many of the nation-wide activities which occur. Who has decided on
what? How do they know what they're doing — how can they be so sure? I
also actively follow the financial news: residential housing outlooks,
prime rate, loans, and GNP."[11] She has learned to use specialized
knowledge, in other words, as a means of interrogating the "text" of the
commonplace, and conversely, she has learned to use her familiar world
as a means of interrogating the wisdom of experts. She has come to see
social life as an ongoing project whose outcome no one can "be so sure"
of; a project, therefore, to which she herself must contribute. Once an
isolated individual living out the cultural script, Lisa now asserts her
willingness — her "right," really her power — to challenge and change the
script.

A teacher, of course, cannot *force* students to accept the "right"
Lisa has claimed, nor can any method reduce to regular steps and
techniques the critical reflection she demonstrates. When Hudson called
for a curriculum that would make such reflection routine, he overlooked
the contradiction inherent in the very idea. To think reflectively is, as
Habermas contends, to suspend the constraints of "strategic" or instrumental reason for the unrestricted exercise of a "communicative"
reason — the former asking "how" from the limited standpoint of disci-

plinary practice, the latter asking "why" from the standpoint of social life as a whole, a life in which everyone has a stake.[12] By turning from Economics to the tangible effects of our economic system, Lisa enters this communicative dimension, this public dimension, where "official" assumptions and methods can be subjected to critical scrutiny. While higher education typically safeguards the authority of its experts by prescribing all such debate from the classroom, Habermas argues that *both* forms of rationality play essential and complementary roles in the work of every discipline. Philosophers never simply "do philosophy," as if their practices needed no further refinement and had no connection to other disciplines or to the larger world. Instead, one aspect of the ordinary practice of philosophers is an interrogation of philosophy itself, and for this reason the history of the discipline is a history of perpetual readjustment to events unfolding outside the enchanted circle of strictly instrumental considerations.

Whereas Hudson had hoped to identify a specific location for public life, an institutional space perhaps distinct from the university, Habermas describes public life as ubiquitous, an *aspect* of social inter-action everywhere, albeit one often obscured or suppressed. He might say that Hudson accepted too readily the mystique of specialization, the idea of a knowledge completely divorced from all extra-disciplinary concerns. Habermas reminds us, by contrast, that knowledge, no matter how theoretical or ostensibly disinterested, is always connected to a larger social world. If Hudson called for a "return" to an undifferentiated public culture, if he perceived the emergence of new languages and practices as a fall from civic grace, Habermas cautions that specialization per se has never been the real problem. He objects, instead, to conven-tional restraints on the uses of knowledge and on our freedom to consider its broader implications. The mystique of specialization has prevented us, he contends, from examining the ways in which knowledge affects our lives and from developing strategies that might allow us to employ it on our own behalf. Hudson presumes that unchecked specialization will diminish the chances for emancipatory social change, but Habermas welcomes specialization as an unprecedented opportunity to enlarge not only our horizons of awareness but also our capacity to act effectively in the world.

Undergraduates like Lisa achieve this capacity, as we have achieved it ourselves, by pursuing a perilous *via media* between uncritical accommodation and an overly critical skepticism, each equally disabling. On the one hand, students must be prepared to resee their familiar worlds from the defamiliarizing perspective of the specialist; on the other hand, they need to keep the familiar world somewhere in view. Anyone who finds Habermas persuasive on the subject of communicative reason will probably agree that students should never be obliged to honor conventionality over truthfulness, or to sacrifice real-world engagement for the sake of a professional decorum. But neither is it possible to transcend these oppositions altogether—to transcend the need for engagement *and* disengagement. Precisely because the public dimension is not a place apart from the academy, nor public language a discourse apart from your way of speaking or mine, the aggressive pragmatism now endorsed by some critics of the status quo, the conviction that learning should forsake abstractions and get down to cases, is every bit as naive as the instrumentalist credo that through a strict adherence to method I can elevate my research above all difference and dissent. Rather than enshrining "knowledge" as a truth superior to the conditions of our actual lives, or conversely, accepting these lives in their present form as the farthest limits of our questioning, we might encourage students to bring formal learning and concrete experience into a relationship of mutual interanimation.[13]

Practice

While the constructionist movement in composition has made the most serious effort thus far to examine the social dimension of knowledge, its proponents still by and large overlook the Balkanized state of the disciplines. Constructionists like Kenneth Bruffee and Patricia Bizzell have merely traded the escapist expressionism of their immediate predecessors for a pedagogy valorizing the normative practices of "communities," by which they mean our all-too-often solitary disciplines and departments.[14] With its connotations of fellowship and shared values, however, the word "community" conceals much more than it reveals. Just as "college life," for the undergraduates Moffatt interviewed, extends beyond the classroom and campus, so an English department is not a community in quite the same sense as a Burmese village, a farming town in the Midwest, or the black Ninth Ward in New Orleans. Even for its most serious practitioners, literary criticism constitutes far, far less than a "world." Indeed, as a discipline (from *dis-*, "apart," and *capere*, "to hold"), criticism must preserve a certain distance from the world. But distance should not be mistaken for disconnection. When constructionists apply the term "community" to disciplines like literary criticism, they lose sight of the larger cultural and historical contexts within which knowledge can become meaningful for our students, and continues to be meaningful for us. It is, after all, the interdependence of text and context—the play of consonance and dissonance between them—that provides the motive force for change in every field, although the seductive illusion of expertise may cause us to forget the academy's dependence on a day-to-day life-world more complex than any method.

Whereas composition pedagogy in the seventies reified the autonomous self, and whereas the constructionists today have reified "communities" as if these were autonomous Selves, monolithic and monological, a pedagogy aimed at making visible the social dimension would teach students how to bring "knowledge" and the world they know into what I have called, after M. M. Bakhtin, mutual interanimation. Such interanimation is the purpose of English 102, the multidisciplinary, research-centered writing course here at Rutgers, which many of our teachers get underway with an essay by Clifford Geertz, "'From the Native's Point of View': On the Nature of Anthropological Understanding." For students and teachers alike, Geertz's essay provides an indispensable point of departure, since it challenges not only the separation of "knowledge" from knowledge but also any attempt to blur their distinctness. "Several years ago," he begins, "a minor scandal erupted" in his discipline: "one of its ancestral figures told the truth." The ancestral figure was Bronislaw Malinowski, first among those who elevated anthropology from travel writing-cum-antiquarianism into the company of respectable social sciences. And the truth Malinowski told was his *Diary in the Strict Sense of the Term*, a work whose posthumous publication gave the lie to his assiduously crafted reputation as a detached observer, "a chameleon fieldworker," in Geertz's words, "self-tuned to his exotic surroundings, a walking miracle of empathy, tact, patience." More high-strung than self-tuned, the real Malinowski struggled "to the point of self-immolation" with the alien values of a culture that his discipline could not lay open automatically. Distancing but not disconnected, his professional training enabled him to frame his experience among the "natives," but this experience *reshaped* his presuppositions in turn. By frankly acknowledging the patriarch's struggle — and the need for struggle — Geertz unveils before his readers the primal scene of all knowledge: calm Reserve in the embrace of an agonized Engagement. Or as he expresses the matter himself somewhat less histrionically: a positioning of the "experience-near" against the "experience-distant."[15]

The communicative reasoning that Habermas merely describes Geertz vigorously enacts in the pages of his essay, where this reasoning assumes the form of a receptivity to the "distant" — to Javanese metaphysics, to Moroccan tribalism, to rival conceptions of anthropology, approached not as raw material or textbook cases but as provisional ways of imagining "ourselves amongst others," of seeing the world through the eyes of others.[16] Even under the pressure of post-modernity, Geertz stubbornly refuses to abandon the "natives" as inscrutable, or else to conclude that when the fieldworker pitches his tent among them he will simply discover what he already "knows." In the absence of foundations, on the contrary, every voice without exception has something meaningful to say. As he enacts it, Geertz's version of communicative reason bears less resemblance to the ideal of pure research — the disciplined application of an impersonal method — than it does to translating a poem or carrying on a conversation, activities through which the contours of the familiar, and the contours of the self in its relation to social life, are redrawn more expansively. Whereas the instrumentalists ask, "What can we do with our knowledge?" Geertz poses an even more basic question: "Who are 'we'?" I would submit that teachers of writing will never restore a social imagination to the classroom unless his question is posed there first — and posed by our students.

Because very few of the students in 102 will earn their livelihoods as anthropologists, we are less concerned with the decorum of that particular "community" than we are with making its specialized knowledge available to nonspecialists, in extra-academic settings. Yet knowledge is never simply available, never simply ready for use at no cost to its users. Consider, for instance, this student's discomfort with Geertz's efforts to explain the Balinese version of selfhood:

> When I first read his essay, I thought that the Balinese' system of birth order names very odd. How can one name a child by a number, not to mention even numbering stillborn children! I can recall my mother, at times, calling out "Child Number Two" when she was in the middle of a busy period and couldn't remember my name. . . . After further reading I seemed to understand that what he suggested was that "births form a circular succession of first, seconds, thirds and fourths in an endless four-stage replication of an imperishable form."
>
> His words "circular succession" illustrated for me images of the Olympic circles that are all connected, or the Ballantine Beer circles which we have all made at one time or another with a sweaty beer glass on a polished mahogany bar. But it also, sadly, brought to mind the recent death of my grandmother. I don't want to believe that my grandmother was just a link in the great chain of history. She was my grandmother. She was supposed to live forever.

In order to determine what selfhood means for the Balinese, or what Geertz means when he talks about the "native's point of view," the writer does not have to concede that her grandmother really was "a link in the great chain of history." But she does need to recognize that something so obvious, so "natural" as the individual's identity might vary

widely from culture to culture. She needs to struggle, like M
with the experience-distant in such a way that the experienc
also be changed. And despite her initial ambivalence, th... change
eventually begins to take place:

> That is the reason why the Balinese idea of imperishable form
> is so disturbing to me. Yes, in theory, or even on paper it appears
> to be fine. But my grandmother was not an actor playing a role in
> this interlocking chain. Yes, I admit that she was linked to her
> mother who was linked further back to my grandmother's mother
> and so on. On the other side she was linked to my mother, who
> links with me and I in turn link with my newborn daughter. I
> know that the chain sounds logical but I don't want to even
> consider my grandchildren's grandchildren referring to my grand-
> mother or even to me as a nameless link in a chain "emerging from
> the worlds of the gods to replace those who, dying, dissolve once
> more into it." Clifford Geertz puts his finger on it when he states:
> "They represent the most time-saturated aspects of the human
> condition as but ingredients in an eternal footlight parade." Were
> George Washington, Albert Einstein, or James Dean nothing but
> mere ingredients? Are we nothing more than faces in museums or
> portraits immortalized in trendy shops? Or worse yet, just a name
> etched on a granite slab?

Even while this writer resists the Balinese view of the person as a
temporary inhabitant of an immutable social role — and even while, I
have the feeling, she would prefer to resist Geertz himself, with his
outlandish digressions and his baffling analogies — her encounter with
anthropology has already begun to transform, and enlarge, the horizon
of her understanding, a horizon she now shares with Geertz, with us,
and with the Balinese, all three formerly "other" to varying degrees.
For better or worse she has been changed, and it is just this disturbing
fact, that real communication irresistibly alters lives and selves by
creating a shared conceptual horizon, that has given instrumentalism,
the myth of a "safe" and impersonal education, its enduring appeal.
Yet papers like the draft above, in their struggle to answer the question
"Who are 'we'?" should reassure us that instrumentalism is indeed no
more than a myth, a collective dream from which one writer in 102,
like Geertz's scandalized anthropologists, has already started to awaken.
If her awakening continues, she will discover what they have discovered
as well: neither a knowledge purged of all particular human intentions,
nor a world made secure from the challenge of the unfamiliar, but a
shared social space, a public space, where each can speak openly to the
other.

Notes

1. Michael Moffatt, *Coming of Age in New Jersey: College and American Culture* (New Brunswick, NJ: Rutgers UP, 1989) 275.

2. Henry Seidel Canby, *American Memoir* (Boston: Houghton Mifflin, 1947) 419.

3. Henry Seidel Canby et al., *English Composition in Theory and Practice* (New York: Macmillan, 1920) 2.

4. Jürgen Habermas, *Toward a Rational Society: Student Protest, Science, and Politics*, trans. Jeremy Shapiro (Boston: Beacon, 1970) 13–14.

5. See, for instance, *Democracy and Education* (New York: Macmillan, 1916; New York: Free Press, 1966) 316–17.

6. Jay William Hudson, *The College and New America* (New York: Appleton Century Crofts, 1920) 53.

7. Hudson 139.

8. Hudson 2–3.

9. Moffatt 40.

10. Moffatt 166.

11. Moffatt 301.

12. Habermas 91–92.

13. I have taken this term from M. M. Bakhtin's "Discourse in the Novel," *The Dialogic Imagination: Four Essays*, ed. Michael Holquist, trans. Caryl Emerson and Michael Holquist (Austin: U of Texas P, 1981) 296.

14. See Patricia Bizzell, "Cognition, Convention, and Certainty: What We Need to Know about Writing," *PRE/TEXT* 3 (1982): 191–207; and Kenneth Bruffee, "Social Construction, Language, and the Authority of Knowledge," *College English* 48 (1986): 773–90.

15. Clifford Geertz, *Local Knowledge* (New York: Basic, 1983) 55–57.

16. Geertz 16.

Reid: I was thinking today, when I was at the one session that I was able to go to, about high school teachers—I don't know a lot of high school teachers who come to 4C's except for the ones who are dying to know exactly what teachers of freshman composition want them to teach. [laughter] And I just was struck with, with the juxtaposition of this discussion coming up tonight, you know about this book. You know, they're not going to be very happy, probably.

Blitz: And college teachers are dying to know "What are high school teachers teaching these students that 'we' keep getting?"

Reid: Yeah, that's what you have, that's what you've said—

Blitz: Nobody's doing very much to actually find out the answers to those questions—

Reid: Yeah, but I think we'd be doing a disservice if we gave "answers."

9

An Interactive Approach to Composition Instruction

Louann Reid
Jeff Golub

Douglas Barnes identifies two learning goals when he says, "The question to be asked is how we can make knowledge available to children without making a strait-jacket of it, how we can increase not minimize children's sense that they can take responsibility for their world, and if necessary change it" (185). Traditional composition instruction, with its emphasis on products, has not provided conditions conducive to accomplishing those goals, and traditional assumptions and institutional structures restrict the changes children and adults can make in their worlds.

Believing that we could improve composition instruction and increase students' sense of responsibility and power, we became interested in creating an interactive classroom. This instructional approach provides a different view of the focus and content and process involved in writing instruction. It is not a series of methods or a guide for teaching. Instead, an interactive classroom emphasizes the centrality of learning through language and provides a context for that learning to occur.

One key assumption of an interactive approach is that collaboration is valuable, an assumption on which this entire book is constructed. The need for and a strong belief in collaboration are the reasons these authors got together in the first place.

The second assumption, that knowledge is constructed, is also evident throughout the chapters and in the roundtable discussions. Marian Yee, for example, talks of the importance of helping students "redefine writing...as acts of intervening in, resisting, and negotiating with those narratives" that construct the students' identities. Cecilia

Rodríguez Milanés describes the ways in which her students constructed their knowledge about authority, community, and the content of the class. Through the discussions we have clarified and reshaped some notions important to this chapter—meanings of resistance, students' reactions to changes, the paradoxes that accompany attempting change under current conditions. Those notions come together when examining the interactive approach to teaching composition.

In its ideal form, an interactive classroom sounds like a pretty good instructional approach. Students talk with each other and with the teacher and learn through a series of experiences. The concept is theoretically sound. Vygotsky supports learning through language use when he says that our language shapes our thought rather than reflects it and when he emphasizes the social nature of learning. Donaldson stresses the importance of using writing to construct meaning. "We do not just sit and wait for the world to impinge on us. We try actively to interpret it, to make sense of it. We grapple with it, we construe it intellectually, *we represent it to ourselves*" (67).

In a classroom where students and teacher subscribe to an interactive approach, we would expect to find a different attitude from that present in a teacher-centered classroom. This attitudinal change would come in part from a change in the teacher's role. He or she would be progressing from information-giver to language-facilitator as described by Charles Suhor:

> The central job of the English teacher is to elicit from students language that helps them to shape and give meaning to their individual experiences and the experiences of others—others whom they meet in the real world and in the imagined worlds of literature. (49)

The teacher in this classroom would rarely be in front of the room. Instead, he or she would serve as a guide for individuals or small groups, constantly moving around the room to ask or answer questions and to offer advice when asked.

For this approach to succeed, the principal or other teacher evaluator would have to believe in it, too. Too often the principal, upon entering classrooms for the purpose of teacher evaluation and seeing students working in small groups, says, "I'll come back when you're teaching something."

However, the ideal rarely happens. In fact, the paradoxes of teaching are never more evident than when we try to implement a change in approach. Look at two more elements of the ideal interactive classroom and the reactions to them.

A change in educational focus would also change students' attitudes toward what is important to know. The teacher would encourage students to focus their attention on *how* they write, realizing that mere construction of knowledge is not enough. Students need to learn how to control their construction of knowledge. After a piece is written, the teacher, in conference with the student or in front of the class with all students, would ask the author to mentally step back and talk about how the piece had been composed. In consciously reconstructing decisions, the student would learn that writing is a matter of making choices and that the good writer knows what choices are available. The student would come to see that writing well does not mean getting it right the first time.

However, this goes against what both students and parents want. The public expects to see clear, correct prose; parents care less about the decisions they cannot see than the misspellings they can. Students do not want to spend time writing and rewriting. They want to get it right the first time and get on with their jobs, their cars, their dates, their other homework.

In the ideal interactive classroom the curriculum would move by experiences, not by objectives. The teacher and the students, not the school board or a committee, would be the curriculum designers, deciding what experiences were appropriate at any particular time. One experience, such as a project to use writing to make a difference to themselves or others, might entail students meeting several objectives such as the ability to write business letters, conduct interviews, write argumentative essays, write letters to editors, and use certain steps to solve a problem. Learning would be integrated, not checked off on a list of mastery skills. Students would write to address something that they had identified as a concern, not to write solely for the teacher's evaluation.

Students resist this approach at first because it seems harder. They ask us just to tell them what we want them to know; they don't want to negotiate the curriculum. Berlin found the same attitude in his university students, who felt that adjusting to the curriculum was best — and good for them, too.

And who can blame students and teachers who do not want to change, who are either comfortable with the system or at least not so uncomfortable that change doesn't seem worse than accommodation? Frankly, we can. Teacher-centered approaches to composition do not encourage true learning, only adjustment to someone else's expectations. We must confront our comfort and, if the paradoxes make us uncomfortable, we need to see what we can change. Everyone involved — teachers, parents, students, administrators — needs to see that an approach that meets the two goals Barnes outlined develops an educated, thoughtful society.

Let's look again at Barnes's two goals — making knowledge available and making students feel responsible. These parallel the two assumptions of the interactive classroom — construction of knowledge and collaboration. In the rest of this chapter we will examine the key questions raised by each assumption, describe the resistance we have seen, and explore what might be done to make each assumption a practical reality in high school classrooms.

Construction of Knowledge

Although "constructing one's own knowledge" makes sense, it is not simple. The key questions are whose knowledge and who controls its construction? Knowledge appears to belong to committees, textbooks, and, occasionally, to teachers. Students are asked to focus their efforts on receiving someone else's knowledge.

Committees divide public school curricula into segments; they may be as broad as English 9, English 10, and so on, or as narrow as "Expository Essay." In writing, the divisions may be "Creative Writing," "Introduction to Essay Writing," "College Preparatory Writing," or other similar titles. These are often decided by a school board, a committee of teachers, a state department, or a university affiliated with the school.

These divisions constrain the types of writing and the purposes for writing that can occur within any class. By separating "creative" from "expository" knowledge, we get the kind of schizophrenic accommo-dation practiced by this student writer.

> Curriculums are geared towards important skills like essay-writing, and usage words. They don't usually care if one knows the entire history of the first, second, and third Dragonlance Wars on Kryun, or of the evil plots of Taphisis, Queen of Darkness to return to Ansalon. But I don't really mind. While I study important stuff at school, I can continue to write about my favorite imaginary places on my own. (Gareth, 1990)

This student has obviously learned what kinds of knowledge he is allowed to construct in his English class.

Another organizational pattern that shapes knowledge but that the student has no control over is tracking, or homogeneous grouping. The more homogeneous the group, the less varied the communication. This doesn't appear to harm upper-level students as much as it does lower because upper-level students already possess a wider range of school knowledge. But classes of low-level students are bound to construct a more limited kind of knowledge about writing if they never see examples that go beyond their own skills. Students with a common background may construct the same meanings and never discover that alternate interpretations exist. They will all be limited by the same language limitations that assigned them to a low-level class in the first place.

Students resist these divisions where possible. In an elective system, students may elect not to take a writing class at all or not to take one that teaches a kind of writing that does not interest them. Many students just do not do assignments that they are not interested in or do the minimum to pass the class. We worry about those getting C minuses, thinking that if we had only taught them better they would receive better grades. But maybe they are doing all they want to on assignments they don't find valuable. Some, like Gareth, accept school learning with resignation. He is resigned to do work that isn't meaningful, but he resists letting it impinge on work he considers important. And the behaviour of disinterested or disenfranchised students is legendary in teachers' lounges, in films, and on the evening news.

Teachers have little power to change the system described so far. However, by constantly questioning the wisdom of such organizational patterns, by using their judgment and knowledge of students to design experiences that will involve the students, and by building on students' talk as a means for learning, some change can occur *within* the system.

Collaboration

Our reading, reflection, and classroom experiences have convinced us that interaction is valuable and necessary. We believe that constructing meanings collaboratively in the classroom helps students become intelligent, responsible citizens, able to use language to accomplish their own purposes. We think that students will come to care about what they are saying and how they are saying it when we offer them experiences and opportunities to interact.

But the current evaluation system, the current daily schedules, and confusion over the teacher's role resist collaboration. The very set of beliefs articulated above, for instance, puts us in conflict with our students. Good students have become good students by finding out what the teacher wants, then delivering it. Look at the questions students ask most frequently of the teacher: "How long does it have to be?" "Is this what you want?" "What can I write about?" They feel that there is no other way to learn and no reason to change. Furthermore, good students resent sharing their knowledge and insights with poorer or lazier students.

All levels of students see writing as an individual, even lonely act. Many students, when asked where they write best, write a variation of this comment:

> Writing in class is really difficult for me. It is hard because I tend to be distracted easily and I do not concentrate as hard as I would alone, away from everyone. Ideas come to me much easier when I am completely alone with no one around to distract me. (Christy, 1990)

Therefore, when the idealistic teacher tries to encourage collaborative composing in class, he or she encounters resistance from students who have learned in any number of previous classes and from any number of cultural influences that writing should be done alone. Students either spend the time socializing, which is what they've learned groups are for, or "collaborating" on their chemistry homework.

We think this resistance keeps students from calling on valuable sources of information—their peers. What can we do in classrooms to show students how valuable their peers are? One attitudinal and practical change we have tried to make is to respond to student requests for feedback only after several other students have read the piece and commented on it. Of course, that puts us in the position of having the student say about a piece we didn't particularly like, "But everyone else liked it a lot." Then where are we? Do we whip out our yardsticks of accumulated reading and writing experience and condemn the ignorance of all the people this student asked, or do we accept the validity of their opinions and explain the reasons for our own? We think that a teacher who believes in interaction will try to take the latter course. It isn't always easy, but we do feel it's important.

Even more worrisome is the idea that our own actions may reinforce the idea that peers are not useful sources. Students immediately discover that their opinions don't *really* count when essays are assessed. As long as the teacher is still the sole evaluator, his or her opinion is the only one that matters. Frankly, this continues to be a sticky problem, whether the teacher believes in transmission or facilitation. One decision we have made is to provide the student with some control by including self-evaluation as a part of the grade. At the end of a major project, we ask students to practice reflective skepticism by writing an essay or letter in which they include answers to several questions. The instructions follow:

> Mentally step back from the project and look at yourself. What have you learned, if anything, from doing this? If you were to do it again, what would you do differently? What aspects of your work on the project pleased you? What aspects displeased you? Include anything you think I should know about your work on this project. What grade do you think you deserve? Why? Tell about yourself in relationship to the project.

One sophomore chose to pursue a project in which she tried to get a major cosmetics company to stop using animals for experiments. She wrote letters and interviewed people in addition to standing by the cosmetics counter in a major department store, discouraging customers from buying that particular brand. She did not succeed in getting testing stopped, but she did use writing both to explain her position and to explore her learning. And her learning was significant. Here's part of her justification for receiving an A.

> I decided that no matter how hard this project was that it was good for me. I learned things about myself I never knew before.
>
> I have always been shy and scared about what people think of me. In a way this project let me "come out of my shell." I stated my beliefs and I stood my ground on them, no matter what other people thought. I didn't back down and that felt great!...
>
> I worked hard and even though I didn't make a huge difference to the world, I made a huge difference to me. I got over a lot of personal barriers and I did what I thought I couldn't, get this done and try hard to (sic). I did a lot of work to (sic). I think it all shows here. (Jenny, 1990)

The depth of this evaluation goes far beyond what a teacher could tell just from the written products. Her self-evaluation counted as half of the final grade. Jenny learned that she could indeed use writing to make a difference. And she learned that her opinion counted not only in animal testing but in assessing learning.

Another effective form of evaluation consistent with an interactive approach involves the students in the setting of the criteria to be used in the evaluation of an assignment. This is similar to the contract approach Cecilia Rodríguez Milanés describes. Having read character sketches written by professional writers and by other students, students draft a character sketch of their own. Then they share their writing in small groups. Finally, the whole class works together to create the criteria for evaluating the papers, using as reference the earlier models and the best qualities of their classmates' writing. This exercise focuses students' attention on the relevant characteristics of good writing and encourages students to reflect on the quality of their own paper. But what if the teacher doesn't feel the criteria that the students generate are stringent enough? We think that's a risk we must take. In our experience, students almost always come up with pretty good criteria. The teacher should be one voice in the discussion, too, so the students are not just trying to guess what criteria the teacher wants them to use. The teacher does not give up total quality control in this or any other assignment, but the discussion that surrounds the selection of criteria often teaches students more about good writing than they would learn in attempting to measure up to criteria selected solely by the teacher or by a textbook publisher.

Besides confusion over the teacher's stance and the problems of evaluation, yet another barrier to collaboration exists in composition classes. There is never enough time — time for students to work with each other, time for teachers to collaborate, and time to meet all of the curricular objectives imposed on the classroom teacher. We haven't found any means to add hours to the day or to buy time. But recognizing that learning takes time, we have tried to reorganize our use of the time we have.

To give students more class time to collaborate and to make that collaboration more effective, we have tried two things. First, we teach students *how* to work in groups. At a minimum, groups need a concrete task, such as brainstorming a list of problems that affect them personally. They also need a recorder and a leader who will report the results to the class or will turn in the assignment. This focus makes the students accountable for their work in small groups and minimizes the amount of chemistry homework that can be done at the same time. We have also rescheduled some of the activities traditionally done during class. Because most students prefer to do their actual writing at home, where they are comfortable and not distracted, we use very little class time for in-class writing and, instead, use it for collaborative prewriting or revising. By selecting the concepts that are most important for students to learn and saving the others in the curriculum guide for "when we have time," we try to ensure that class time is used for collaboration, not individual work that could better be completed elsewhere. But we would like to have more class time. Some discussions barely get going well before the bell rings.

Time for teachers is more difficult to find, and we have no easy answers. Administrators are reluctant to commit the money necessary to give teachers release time to work together, and the need to be sure that all students are supervised at all times makes scheduling teacher time together more difficult. But we must insist that teacher collaboration is vital to the future of education. Professionals should not be doing hall duty or watching bathrooms for sneaky smokers. Using teachers this way is a costly pseudosolution to an administrative problem. It would be more cost-effective to hire aides or request parent volunteers for those nonacademic duties and free teachers to work on educational issues.

Dialogue between teachers at all levels and across levels is essential. If teachers are part of an electronic network, some collaboration can be obtained through bulletin boards or electronic mail. Attending state and national conferences offers a chance to hear what colleagues are saying and doing. Reading journals also helps facilitate some cross-level sharing. But the fact is that there is no alternative to dialogue, to asking each other questions. The irony of our approach in the system we currently have is that it is difficult to have an interactive classroom without interacting!

The problems for students and teachers might be lessened by a daily schedule that encourages collaboration and allows more time for constructing knowledge. For example, one of our schools plans a radically different schedule next year. Students will attend a particular class every other day for eighty-five minutes, rather than attending every day for fifty-three. Although there will be a net loss of minutes over the semester, students should be able to concentrate more on the three or four classes they have each day instead of being expected to mentally shift gears every hour, six times a day. Productive time will be increased by minimizing the number of times each day that teachers take attendance and get students settled down. Teachers will be able to schedule a common planning period by department if they choose, gaining time for collaboration. Although not a panacea for all problems that plague schools, this solution should not cost more money and may give students and teachers the time they so badly need to improve education.

Unfortunately, this could turn into another cosmetic change. Unless we examine the deep structural assumptions that guide our teaching and prohibit interactive approaches, no significant change will occur. Teachers who believe that the goal of education is to transmit the collective knowledge of Western civilization will still use transmission approaches. They may well try to lecture for eighty-five minutes, feeling compelled to "cover" more curriculum in less time. And unless teachers force administrators to change their assumptions about teachers' roles, such a schedule could just provide more time for teachers to patrol the restrooms.

We hope that this schedule change will create both the necessity and the opportunity for teachers to talk together, to plan, to examine their assumptions together, in short, to collaborate before the next school year begins. We also hope, perhaps naively, that these discussions will affect the problems associated with what we see as the largest resistance to the two goals we set forth earlier — curricular pressures.

In some districts, teachers must teach a curriculum they may not even have designed. School boards can veto aspects of a curriculum they do not like. In some schools, a teacher is evaluated on how much of the curriculum she is able to cover in a set period of time. Even when the pressure is not that extreme, teachers feel they need to teach as much as possible in the time they have. Although this is a worthy goal, "coverage" does not seem to be particularly effective, especially in teaching writing. Students need time to practice, to experiment, to explore. Thus, we prefer to see our jobs as helping students "uncover" the curriculum rather than covering it for them and hoping they will learn. This means offering some long-term projects such as the one mentioned earlier.

There are no easy answers to the problems of change in high school composition instruction. However, by examining the forces of resistance to both traditional instruction and to an approach designed to improve instruction, teachers can take responsibility for change and can increase their students' feelings that they, too, have some control over their knowledge and how they obtain it. Barnes emphasizes,

> A culture which reduces pupils to passive receivers of knowledge is likely to reduce teachers to passive receivers of curricula, and to deny them the time and resources that would enable them to take active responsibility. (188)

Teachers must be the first to take responsibility for change. Informed, reflective practitioners can improve conditions for composition and composition instruction. Because of and despite the resistance we encounter, we must continue to re-examine our assumptions and our practice.

Note

We want to thank the other members of the Baltimore and Chicago roundtables for the ideas their comments stimulated. This chapter would not have been written in its present form without them. We are especially grateful to Michael and Mark for their sensitive, insightful editing. They forced us to examine assumptions we didn't even realize we held and, in so doing, helped us to see more clearly what we know and believe.

Works Cited

Barnes, Douglas. *From Communication to Curriculum*. Harmondsworth, England: Penguin Books, 1975.

Donaldson, Margaret. *Children's Minds*. New York: W. W. Norton, 1978.

Suhor, Charles. "Content and Process in the English Curriculum." *Content of the Curriculum*. Ed. R. S. Brandt, ASCD Yearbook. Alexandria, VA: Association for Supervision and Curriculum Development, 1988. 31–52.

Gareth, Christy, and Jenny are students at Douglas County High School, Castle Rock, Colorado.

Hurlbert: I actually attended a good panel today [CCCC Chicago 1990]. A good one. Sara-Hope Parmeter, from the University of California Santa Cruz, who teaches developmental writers, and Debbie Bell [Ohlone Elementary, Freedom, CA], a teacher of fifth graders, both teach large populations of multiethnic students. And they both knew they couldn't teach them to think critically—they don't share the culture of the students they're teaching, and they don't want to set themselves up as experts. So, they started shipping each other's class to visit the other one. So, the college students were visiting the fifth graders. The fifth graders were going over to the campus to visit the college students. And the college students wrote books, produced these incredible books for these fifth graders—incredible graphics, stuff in Spanish and English, bilingual texts. The fifth graders were getting these, and they started writing back. They made books to send back to the college students. And, of course, they were finding out lots of, you know, lots of wonderful composition things about audience and all that. But they were doing a lot more interesting things than that. There was this one guy, for instance, who actually survived street gang life in LA, who wrote his book with one particular fifth grader in mind, and he wrote this book about life in a street gang and drugs and police and the kind of life you lead. And when I was looking at this book, and holding it in my hand, I could *see* a significant social action. And there was real power in this book. That's the kind of stuff I want to hear about and talk about and find out a lot more about. I want to know about options, things I can do to really make a difference where *I* am. Because the difference I'm going to make is creating a situation where other people make the differences for themselves.

Spellmeyer: Don't you think that that's a healthy commitment? Because it's— you have an ideal of open communication, but you don't know how it's going to be realized. And I don't think we have, we're not wallowing in relativism, right now. I think that we all want that. We just don't know how to realize it. And I think that's a mature theoretical attitude.

Yee: That's a really good story.

Hurlbert: It's a terrific—oh, they were *so* great, they were doing good things, and telling us good things.

Yee: What I like about that is that there is active participation, there's direct contact with the audience, and there's also very limited, probably very limited, there's probably just one audience or just one classroom. I mean it's temporary. A couple of people read it, and it was gone. But, it had a significant impact. I guess in relation to *this* book [*Composition and Resistance*], I don't think we need to worry too much about whether, or how much of an impact this book is going to have. I mean, I kind of like the idea of something written for the moment. Having a limited impact, and then moving on. I think there's something necessary about things having short-lived lives and then ideas transforming, taking another shape and going on.

Singleton: Let's see, that relates to what Nancy was saying when she says she does this for herself to come here and talk to people in a conversation. A conversation can be valid. You know things that are valid don't have to be measured on time scales, necessarily. And if our conversation is a valuable experience for you [Nancy] then maybe this wider conversation of the book may be a momentary, valid experience for someone else. And [it] may lead to other conversations, which is what sounds like is already happening. And extending the conversation—that, in itself, is a change, you know, those conversations can change people. I see what Jim Sledd's saying about maybe not revolutionary change, but I guess I like to believe that revolutionary changes come about from the small beginning of a conversation that leads to another conversation that leads to another conversation that leads to another. So change and bringing up questions in people's minds starts a chain reaction.

Mack: Aronowitz had a model for this that he mentioned at his conference. He was talking about working with students and having a lot of conversations. And he said what you do—this is very premeditated—is to sit around and wait for the administration to make a mistake. And then when you're talking all the time, you can mobilize more quickly. And we were trying in the one session late this afternoon to talk about "Where's the profession going?" and "Are there going to be jobs?" and "Is there going to be a shortage of Ph.D.s?" and people were saying "Yes" and some people were saying "No." We can't predict all those things, but I think if we continually question, we can be ready to go into action at moments that are important. This happens at our own institutions all the time. I mean you get some piece of drivel in your mailbox that says, in my institution, that "we want to move toward 400 people in a section of General Education classes because we'll better serve students," and that happens one day, and then you have to respond. You can't really predict what kinds of confrontations you are going to have. But you, we, have to be questioning all the time so that you're ready to move into action, because that's what teaching is. Teaching is being with a group of people in a room and something happens, gets put on the table, and you have to deal with it.

Reid: But what makes people want to question? I think we're back to the uncomfortable student issue again. Kids don't want to question. They don't want somebody questioning them. They want to get it and spit it back, and they want that for a good reason, I mean, we have taught them to do that. But if questioning is indeed valuable, and I agree it is, then what can we do in order to make that not be a confrontive or abrasive or negative action? Or an action where *we're* holding the power and the questions. And make them *want* to question.

Singleton: But is it so much a matter of wanting to question? Sitting around wanting to question? It seems like it doesn't happen that way. Something happens and then you react to it. It's not "I'm looking for a question to get all excited about." Something happens that bothers me, that irritates me, that I can't put up with so then I want to take some action. I want to say, "No." And I don't think our students, they're not looking for questions, but they have things that come upon them that they have to react to, negatively, positively—

Reid: So our curriculum should be a series of irritants? [laughter]

Reid: I didn't mean that in a nasty way!

Singleton: I'd say it has to be, it will be. I mean, life is that way. Things happen that—

Harris: I agree with that. I mean, my sense is that, I would describe students as not so much as they don't want to question as, really, the opposite. They strike me as generally intellectually curious. And I think that a peculiar thing about school is that it strikes them that, it teaches them often that, the things they're curious about and the kinds of knowledge and expertise they have are inappropriate or largely uninteresting. So I mean the first thing—a zillion people have said this, but I mean if you want to prime curiosity, you ask them about things that have some kind of relevance and use within their lives. And you ask them, well, I'll stop there.

Spellmeyer: I really like what you're saying [Singleton], and I agree with Joe because, I mean, this is another kind of cultural inheritance that we have to beware of, and it goes back to the whole tradition of disinterested thought. So that theory is, you say, "Well, what shall I question?" Right? As though you had no human interest, but of course you [Blitz] said there are people sleeping on the streets. Our society is riddled with contradictions. And the lives of our students are riddled with contradictions. It's true that those tend to get, those tend to be read out or those tend to be glossed over, but students are quite aware of them as you're [Harris] saying. And it doesn't take much, I think, to— it's not an imperial—you're not dominating them simply to point out, you know, "this is true and yet this is true and yet these are contradictory, what do you make of that?" and let *them* make something of that. But there's so many of these—

Singleton: And I didn't question that we have to bring it up to them. I think that if we allowed them, they would bring [questions] up, but something has happened with school. Human beings are normally curious. You know, sit in a room with a two-year-old child or a three-year-old child and they are curious about things. When we take them into the schoolroom, we tell them to sit down and be quiet and not move. That's when they learn that that place is not a place for learning and for being curious because you get in trouble. We have curtailed the normal human trait of being curious, so then we have to make up *assignments* to make them curious again about the things that we *want* them to be curious about. We really do an insane thing here.

Mack: Yeah, see the assumption is, once again, what the students don't know. What they know is that they can't ask these questions in front of you because it's not polite, but under their breath, and in the back of the room and out in the hallway, they question all kinds of stuff about what's going on in that classroom.

10

Teaching for Literacy in Socio-Cultural and Political Contexts

Miriam T. Chaplin

What Is Literacy?

At its most basic level, literacy is an instrument of the social order that facilitates communication between members of particular social groups. But, as Robert Pattison contends, literacy is not merely communication. Literacy is also behavior that exhibits a consciousness of the problems and uses of language and the ability to express this consciousness in ways evolved and sanctioned by the group (6).

Standards are implicit in all considerations of literacy and it is because of its standards that literacy becomes politically significant. Standards of literacy foster the formation of status and power relationships within groups. Standards, however, are not absolute. They are more often than not arbitrary decisions made by those who hold powerful positions and the standards set by these persons help to sustain their power. The status of inclusion is conferred upon those who conform to the standards, and those who do not conform, often for reasons beyond their control, are excluded. Thus, the standards of literacy are at the same time effective means of oppression and liberation.

The academic community is a social group that sets its own standards of literacy and requires students to conform to them. Students who can exhibit conformity to academic standards become members of an inner circle often referred to as the mainstream of a college community. Students who are unwilling or unable to conform may be afforded the opportunity to enroll in college, but it is likely that they will experience feelings of dislocation and exclusion because they must operate on the fringes of the mainstream.

Most of these nonmainstream college students are in the mainstream of other social groups to which they belong. Indeed, it may be their leadership status in those groups that stimulates their desire to enter college. It does not take long, however, for nonmainstream students to realize that there is an ambivalence between the perception of their abilities outside of college and the way these abilities are perceived by the institution. At the very beginning of their college careers, non-mainstream students must learn to cope with this ambivalence. They must strike a balance between what they already know and what they are expected to learn. It is often a difficult task.

Within the academy, however, these students are assisted in their efforts by zealous teachers who understand that academic literacy is an alternative literacy rather than a standard for all other kinds. These are the teachers who employ instructional techniques that acknowledge students' individual abilities as well as the collective histories from which those abilities evolved. In most instances, these are also the teachers who are aware of the critical issues that impinge upon the teaching of literacy in American colleges and universities. This discussion will highlight three focal points around which many of these issues cluster: diversity, vocationalism and competition.

Diversity

Jean Lewis is a 25-year-old African American female. Jean has worked in a beauty shop for three years. She is now enrolled in a state university where she hopes to obtain a degree in English as well as certification for high school teaching. Jean made high scores in reading and English composition in her placement tests. She is enrolled in English Composition 102. Jean's reading interests may be considered narrow. She enjoys stories about movie and television stars, but she does not follow current events and is easily bored with any content that is historical in nature.

Myron Boning is a 36-year-old Irish American male who worked as a roofer until he was injured on the job and was forced to find other employment. Myron is enrolled in a state university and has selected computers as his major course of study. His math skills are very strong, and he is an avid reader. His scores on the English Placement test were below average, and he was placed in a basic composition course.

Maria Romero is a 19-year-old Hispanic American female. Maria was born in America, but has spent the last ten years in Puerto Rico. The family has just moved back to the United States, and Maria is enrolled in a community college. She hopes to earn an Associate Degree and transfer to a four-year institution. Maria speaks both English and Spanish, but she has considerable problems reading and writing in both languages. She is placed in a basic composition course and in developmental reading.

Before the 1960s, students like Jean Lewis, Myron Boning, and Maria Romero might not have considered a college education an alternative. However, as a result of civil rights legislation in 1965, colleges and universities began to enroll increased numbers of racial and ethnic minorities, women, and older students. The transformation in college populations in the last three decades is similar only to the land grant movement of the late 1800s. As was true in the 1800s, the recent democratization has led to extensive discussions about the purpose of higher education and its ability to educate students whose interests, goals, and abilities are as divergent as their sociocultural histories. What should an institution offer its students and what should students bring to the academic experience?

Attempts to answer this fundamental question have consumed the attention of institutional administrators, faculties, the business community, and state legislatures. A viable answer depends to a great extent on the amount and kind of student population diversity in the institution. The question loses some of its significance when applied to institutions whose students are more alike than different.

No institution, however, has escaped the scathing criticism aimed at higher education in the last ten years for its failure to respond adequately to the question of diversity. The criticism has ranged from a call for more instruction in communication skills to increased emphasis on humanities. Several national status-of-education reports have targeted higher education and urged reforms. The reports differ in their recommendations, but they unanimously support an emphasis on critical thinking that encourages students to actively interpret content rather than passively receive it.

Most teachers of literacy agree that students should develop the ability to think beyond the concrete level of content material. They face the problem, however, of helping students like Maria Romero, Myron Boning and Jean Lewis to develop the necessary basic skills, to employ higher thinking strategies, and to internalize content in the limited time available to them. If, with the Maria Romeros, the focus is exclusively on a development of basic skills, such students may not broaden their range of knowledge. If, with the Jean Lewises, there is a concentration on content acquisition, the critical thinking skills may go undeveloped. With all students, teachers must be concerned with the connections that instruction makes to the students' lives. Students, especially those outside of the mainstream, do not respond favorably to instruction that fails to consider their prior experiences or present interests.

Therefore, the teaching of literacy is more than a decision to embrace a pedagogy of skills or a pedagogy of knowledge. Skills and knowledge must be emphasized simultaneously, for it is not one or the other but learners on whom instruction should be focused. Teaching is enhanced when, as Maxine Greene says, "students are brought into the negotiation of meanings" (239).

Placing students rather than curriculum in the center of instruction is a perspective that differs greatly from that espoused by Allan Bloom and E. D. Hirsch—the proponents of cultural literacy. Hirsch's list of terms "that every literate American should know" and Bloom's insistence on a strong foundation in the knowledge of the history and literature of western civilization seems to imply that a specific brand of knowledge supersedes concern with learners. Teachers whose classrooms contain diversified learners, however, must reject the positions of Bloom and Hirsch. These teachers must proceed from the position that the value of knowing does not reside in knowledge but in the cognitive and emotional underpinnings that determine how learners will use the knowledge they acquire. Literacy must be viewed as a means of liberating students instead of indoctrinating them. Teachers must be influenced by Baldwin Ransom's contention that "no information is intrinsically valuable, but gains significance as it is relevant to particular inquiries" (28).

The centrality of language to literacy places composition teachers in the vanguard of literacy education. Whatever students' cultural orientations, knowledge bases, or skill levels, composition teachers are expected to harness the chameleon called "literacy" and share it with every student. This is a charge of ever widening proportions and the success that teachers have in responding to it is directly related to their understanding of language as a social construct that makes literacy possible for all students.

Vocationalism

Most college students today, mainstream and nonmainstream alike, enter college with clearly defined career goals. The mainstream students may be the offsprings of second, third, and even fourth-generation college graduates. These students may have had the advantage of early training and preparation for their schooling and their life's work. Thus, they may be following a meticulous agenda and may have carefully calculated or estimated the time it will take to attain their goals. Students in this group are likely to consider an undergraduate education a necessary precondition for graduate and professional study that will ultimately lead to a position of economic security and influence.

The nonmainstream students, on the other hand, are more often representative of the working class of American society, and their lives are quite different from their mainstream counterparts. These students may not have had a support system of assistance and encouragement along the way. It is highly likely that the racial minorities in this group bear deep wounds inflicted by racist practices and attitudes encountered in the workplace and in the schools. Working-class white students may have escaped racial prejudices, but it is unlikely that they have escaped class or gender discrimination. As a result of these experiences, the attitudes of most working-class students toward college work is one of urgency. They want to acquire education credentials that they believe will lead to gainful employment and an improved life-style, and they want to do this as efficiently as possible. Learning for learning's sake is a luxury that working-class students feel they cannot afford. Through the process of education, they may acquire a range of knowledge in the academic disciplines, but this is not their primary reason for attending college.

The vocational orientation of college students is of great concern to those who favor liberal learning. While many college faculties turn away from the extreme positions of Bloom and Hirsch, they support the idea that a liberal foundation of knowledge is a necessary goal in higher education. These faculties fear that the practicality in college curriculums that students desire threatens the integrity of a college degree. The Association of American Colleges and the Carnegie Foundation refer to students' vocational preoccupation and the effect that it is having on institutions:

> Today's student populations are less well prepared, more vocationally oriented, and apparently more materialistic than their immediate predecessors. College administrators are required, at the peril of losing their jobs and their institutions, to pay attention to the peculiar characteristics of each generation of students. (Association of American Colleges, 1985, p. 5)

> The curriculum is more strongly oriented than ever before toward the consumer and toward the provision of consumer "durable goods" to be enjoyed over a lifetime. (Carnegie Foundation for the Advancement of Teaching, 1978, p. 4)

Working-class students are more often the targets of these criticisms because they are the students who offer the most resistance to a traditional liberal curriculum. The students' resistances, however, are often grounded in real-world experiences and awareness of the contradictions and limitations of a traditional education. Working-class students are aware of people who are unemployed, incarcerated, and/or on public assistance who have earned baccalaureate degrees. They can also point to persons who have risen to powerful positions of wealth and influence in society with a minimum amount of formal learning. These observations do not deter students from their goal of obtaining education credentials. They know that credentials are important to economic upward mobility for the vast number of Americans. However, most working-class students are interested in obtaining credentials that will pay the greatest dividends in the least amount of time.

This cost-efficient attitude is not limited to college students. It is the orientation of Americans generally. In America, money is power, and working-class students, particularly, are seeking an escape from the powerlessness that has characterized their own lives and those in their families for generations before them.

Yet, these students continue to face the scourge of powerlessness in the academic world. The powerlessness is most evident in the system of standardized testing which makes students victims of test scores. The scores that students make on these tests determine where they will be placed and what they will be taught. The pervasiveness of testing in higher education and its adherence to a deficiency model that identifies students' weaknesses rather than their strengths is often referred to as the covert gatekeeper of social and economic mobility which replaces the overt constraints of earlier times. It institutionalizes an established conservative agenda by separating the haves from the have-nots (those with high scores and those with low scores). It is not surprising then that students have a disrespect and disdain for standardized tests and offer resistance to the courses that they are required to take as a result of them.

Students' resistant attitudes spread beyond basic skills courses into the academic disciplines where they meet a similar resistance on the part of teachers. A knowledge of students' placements in remedial and developmental courses leads some teachers to expect low performances in their classes and this expectation is evident in their attitudes toward instruction. Such teachers long for the more traditional students of former years. Indeed, working-class students complain that there are teachers who spend entire semesters lost in nostalgic trances from which they teach generations of students who are no longer in their classes.

In most cases, students must endure this disrespect. Whenever possible, however, they use the resources available to them to demand change to a more humanistic education. Student resistance to traditional education and their demands for practicality is a form of political action and according to Richard Shaull, political action is a positive sign of literacy. He writes:

> Education either functions as an instrument which is used to facilitate integration into the logic of the present system and bring conformity

to it or it becomes the 'practice of freedom' the means by which men and women deal critically and creatively with reality and discover how to participate in the transformation of their worlds" (15).

The resistances of students to the repression they feel in higher education implies that they may be more politically astute and in touch with methods used in the mainstream of American life than their low-status classifications in college imply. While these students may lack specific academic skills, working-class students have learned the lessons that a materialistic society has taught them. The vocational pre-occupation that students display is a sign that they have learned these lessons well.

Competition

Competition is the hidden curriculum in American schools. It begins to be taught as soon as students enter school and it intensifies as they move through the educational system. In the early grades, students learn to compete for a place in the "top group." In the upper grades, the higher track is the enviable position. The competition between teachers who desire to teach the more advanced classes in elementary and secondary schools is no less fierce than that of the students who desire to be in them.

However, the competition in lower levels of education seems like small game when compared to competition in higher education. The manner in which different parts of an institution compete with each other is described by Alexander Astin:

> Academic departments compete with each other over FTES and funding, academic personnel compete with student affairs personnel over a finite resource pie, and trustees and administrators compete with faculty for control over resource-allocation decisions (15).

Competition is not limited to intra-college affairs; institutions compete with each other for resources that protect their ranking as "quality" institutions. This is a round-robin kind of competition, which Alexander Astin describes as a reputation/resource view of education. According to Astin, "having more resources enhances reputation and a good reputation helps to bring in more resources." Astin offers an alternative view of education which he calls a "cooperative talent development view" in which institutions would base their reputation on their ability to affect students in a positive way.

While Astin's rational alternative to the reputation/resource view is antithetical to the dominant values in American society — material possessions determine quality and worth — they are not far removed from the changing nature of competition in corporate America. Corporations that once competed with each other are now forming monopolies or conglomerates that give them control over larger territories of wealth. These corporations are realizing that individual competition has its limits.

A similar move in higher education could positively influence some of its practices. If colleges and universities attempted to form a monopoly for education rather than competing with each other, they might garner more resources. More importantly, they could share the common goal of developing the potential of students regardless of which institution they attended. If this cooperative view permeated all parts of institutions, there could be positive changes in the way higher education is designed and practiced.

First, a change in the current philosophy underlying institutional practices could eliminate forced conformity to standards that are developed apart from the learners to which they apply. Indeed, the very concept of standard could be replaced by a concept of alternative. Literacy could then be viewed in a broader connotation that is elastic enough to incorporate many different kinds of skills and knowledge. Second, it could foster the belief that literacy is a social practice rather than an individual cognitive act. College classes could become communities of learners where teachers create an environment for learning instead of stations of indoctrination. This could change the popular one-directional method of instruction in which students vie for the highest grade based on the best regurgitation of the information contained in the teacher's lecture and the course textbook.

Third, a philosophical change could foster the concept of interpersonal evaluation as it relates to group efforts. Evaluation could depend on the process used by student groups to arrive at viable solutions instead of individual students' attempts to provide correct answers to pre-digested questions. Students would, thus, realize that there are few correct answers to problem situations, but there are many solutions. Communicating and utilizing the talents of the group members is the way to arrive at the most workable solution. This kind of cooperative and collaborative learning celebrates different perspectives and could help students to learn from each other as well as the teacher.

Some of these practices currently occur in isolated classrooms, but they are considered to be techniques used for teaching — not for living in the academic world. When the teachers who use them leave their classrooms, they must abandon their cooperative ideas and enter the competitive world of the institution. They must compete for their share of departmental resources, and in most institutions, these resources are limited.

Composition teachers are responsible for the literacy education courses (writing and, in some cases, reading), and these courses require huge allocations of personnel. English departments rarely have enough full-time faculty to staff these courses, so they employ large numbers of part-time faculty. The use of part-time faculty to teach developmental courses is a political arrangement of the highest order.

It creates a labor force of second class citizens (in most cases women), and it minimizes the importance of literacy education by relegating it to persons who are disenfranchised by their nonmembership status and who receive none of the benefits of a faculty appointment.

The precariousness of the position can affect the quality of instruction that part-time teachers provide. If part-time teachers are persons who have no desire to make teaching a full-time career, they may be uninformed about new teaching methods or advances in the field of knowledge. The institution provides no research support or financial incentives for their professional development. Unless these part-time teachers are willing or financially able on their own to become acquainted with new pedagogy in order to respond better to the needs of their students, they may be sensitive to students' needs but too uninformed to do much about them.

If part-time teachers are graduate students, their first commitment is to their own education. When students complete their degrees, part-time work may be the only academic positions available. Therefore, students vie for them. As a part-time teacher, these graduates, like nonmainstream students, live on the edges of their profession rather than in its center.

Yet, with all of the problems involved in offering composition and other developmental courses, academic departments still compete for control of them. Literacy education is considered to be a drain on precious resources, but the bountiful FTES that the courses generate make the competitive effort worthwhile. All too often, literacy courses in institutions of higher learning are political pawns in a game in which the rules are made neither by the teachers who teach them nor by the students who take them.

Works Cited

Association of American Colleges. *Integrity in the College Curriculum: A Report to the Academic Community*. February 1985.

Astin, Alexander. "Competition or Cooperation" *Change* (September/October, 1987): 15.

Bloom, Alan. *The Closing of the American Mind*. New York: Simon & Schuster, 1987.

Carnegie Foundation for the Advancement of Teaching. *Missions of the College Curriculum*. San Francisco, Jossey-Bass, 1978.

Greene, Maxine. "Expanding the Range of Literacy" *English Education* 18.4 (1986): 239.

Hirsch, E. D. *What Every Literate American Needs to Know* Boston: Houghton Mifflin, 1987.

Pattison, Robert. *On Literacy*. New York: Oxford UP, 1982.

Ransom, Baldwin. "Questioning the Meaning of Literacy." *Education Week*. 6. 31 (1987): 28.

Shaull, Richard. Foreword to Paulo Freire's *Pedagogy of the Oppressed*. New York: Seabury, 1968.

11

The Feminization of Literacy

J. Elspeth Stuckey

> Why should you have to be the same as a man to get what a
> man gets simply because he is one?
>
> Catherine MacKinnon

The idea of feminist literacy may seem odd as opposed to the idea of cultural literacy, which may not. This is a matter of culture, not feminism, and culture is hardly fair. Culture, in fact, is a feminist fight, in spite of a rather fanciful view of culture as redemption. To invade culture is perhaps the primary purpose of feminism and certainly a chief concern of feminist literacy.

Barbara Smith, in the introduction to *Home Girls: A Black Feminist Anthology*, gives us an example of the conflict. She says, "To me the phrase 'Act like you have some sense,' probably spoken by at least one Black woman to every Black child who has ever lived, is a cryptic warning that says volumes about keeping your feet on the ground and your ass covered" (xxiv). It is a phrase of survival, yet it is double-edged. Disfranchised people had better cover up, but the more they cover, the less others see. On a broad scale, this is the situation women occupy. Yet the scattering and fragmentation of women from each other, most particularly minority women from majority women, persists, under cover...under culture. Catherine MacKinnon sums up the dilemma precisely. "What we are forever wondering," she asks, "is whether there's anything *other* than the reality of the world men make" ("Desire" 113).

Our question — how women and literacy interact — is thus contingent upon both the interaction of women and men and of women and women. James Sledd provides a partial answer in his essay in this collection. He says that standardized language [literacy] is purposefully imposed by a dominant, centralized, national power. The dominating, centralizing powers of which he speaks are those of white, Anglo, middle- and upper-class, profit-minded men who control the modes of literacy acceptable to the economy and to the satisfaction of male income. Once one discovers the axis of salary, the axis of literacy emerges. What Sledd fails to appreciate is that the perpetuation and stabilization of male control is not accomplished by men but by the women they employ. Indeed, the standardization of literacy in America and the mass exploitation it entails are ensured by women. Women, who make up over 80 percent of the teaching workforce in the United States at a much diminished level of recompense, exploit those who would be literate — small, poor children, adolescent troublemakers, teenage mothers, out-of-work textile spinners, maids, and laid-off city garbage collectors. The irony, of course, is that this is something only women can admit. Men cannot say something like this — for good reason. Certainly, James Sledd could not — and would not — say it. Yet there the truth is in front of us. The major questions we must address, then, are why women in literacy do not say the truth; why they do much of which is not in their best interest; why they have a stake in a system that is killing them; how, within the practices of literacy, women perpetuate the exploitation of the weakest members of society, among whom they number?

The clearest reason, of course, is that a literate economy exploits those who would be women, also. The everydayness of the exploitation is its strongest feature. For example, if asked to describe their positions in educational hierarchies, most women would describe situations of powerlessness. They would speak of bureaucracy, senseless paperwork, senseless textbooks and assignments, boredom, disciplinary problems, sexism, burn-out, and the uncertainty of the future. The situation of the lower level college literacy teacher, known often as the lecturer, the composition teacher, or the entry-level instructor is typical. (The situation for teachers of K−12 is as compelling, though certain states today pay public school literacy teachers better salaries than college personnel.) Here is a description: Women teach most of the entry-level composition courses, remedial/developmental/noncredit English courses, "advanced" composition courses, introductory literature courses, and study-skill-type courses in colleges in America. Many of these women teach part time. Many of them teach overloaded classes. Many of them are highly over-qualified. The wages are subsistence, and many women still make less than men employed in comparable positions (though certainly many institutions are committed to the same low adjunct wages for women and men). A sizeable workforce of women is employed in units of three or five years to teach these courses and then fired, never having been put on tenure track and never having been professionally recognized. Often, these women are hired or fired on the first or last day of college registration if classes make or do not make. It is possible to teach two composition courses at a large, respectable, private Midwestern college today and to earn $639 a month. State-run colleges in the South pay $1,500 per part-time composition course. It is possible to earn considerably less at other institutions.

This does not even address what women do in the classroom. What they do is often dictated and overseen by directors of literacy who are usually men, but, more trenchantly, men who have demonstrated that they can be team players. This tradition is inscribed in day-to-day syllabi and evaluated on arbitrary, numerical scales. Most entry-level literacy instructors spend their time grading essays whose numbness is the single reason a numbed instructor can get through them. It is hyperbolic but not ahistorical to compare the textile mill piecework of women in the early twentieth century with the home essay grading of literacy teachers in the latter part of the century. More damning is that the very women who have had to feed the children they're minding have had to relegate to insufficient economic entitlement the bottom of the population they desperately seek to avoid becoming themselves.

Dorothy Dinnerstein provides an apt overlay of this situation. She describes the laws that govern the daily interactions of men and women. "Inside certain class and caste limits," she says,

> a man is entitled to issue blunt orders, contradict people flatly, instruct or command or forbid outright, respond without apology or circumlocution. Another man is entitled to respond in kind; if he is less powerful, physically or socially, it can be unwise for him to do so, but it is not unmanly; indeed, it can enhance his standing. A woman may offer some countersuggestion or protest to the substance of the man's pronouncement, but she must not reject in principle his right to make it, nor may she claim the same kind of right for herself. If she breaks this rule—except in an experimental contest of strength, which she hopes he will win—she can expect trouble. And if another woman addresses her in the spirit that she takes for granted in him, that woman in turn can expect trouble from her (177).

This description is certainly not unfamiliar to women who have ever attended a teachers' meeting. Men run education; education runs literacy; literacy runs women. Women run.

Yet Dinnerstein introduces a troubling point. Women, she implies, exploit other women. In fact, as she says, a woman who acts like a man "can expect trouble." And, of course, she is right. In literacy instruction, the exploitation of women by women is a daily occurrence.

Yes, women are historical victims. But why do they continue to condone the system that subordinates them?

The chief reason is that women have no choice. Women have historically taken the worst jobs because that is all they could get. In women's jobs, women have competed with women. And, in the academic case, the worst English teaching job is certainly better than a lot of jobs women have had to take.

Another reason has to do with who or what a woman is. Whether "naturally" or "socially" maternal (and the dichotomy itself is subversive), women seem to be women-bound to help others. A woman may be a victim, but at least she can help others to escape being victimized. Thus, women in literacy find themselves (tokenly) responsible for the livelihoods of American students. And women respond on cue. Good women can handle the burden, or at least they will go down trying. Bad women will simply fail to meet up to good-woman standards.

A third reason is that men want women to think that women's responsibility for others is a natural state. Many women in literacy, in fact, are supported by men who finance this argument. This is perhaps the most insidious reason. The truth is that many, many women in literacy are comfortable enough to see little or no reason to change things. Often the women who occupy the lowest positions in English departments or who labor in marginal public K−12 school conditions and shoulder the largest burdens can afford to stick. These women are often wives or single women without children. They can pay the bills and save a little money and go on summer vacations — or contribute to mortgages, college educations, and car payments. They can do this and watch other women bear the brunt of an unequal society but never have to do much about it. Literacy is a "woman's job." As awful as the situation gets, women endure it, comply with it, perpetuate it, make busy the businesslike. If they did not, the situation simply could not exist.

Yet if such a statement sounds suspiciously like a case of blaming the victim, it is. Whereas it is necessary for women to stop seeing themselves as victims, it is the baldest truth that they are victims right now and that the victims are responsible not only for not saving themselves but for not saving the literacy of many of the nation's students, most especially the minority and the poor students. Women, indeed, are guilty.

But, then, women are always guilty; it is a useful state for them to be in. It is certainly one they are used to. The chief question is why women continue to bear the guilt, or, to put it another way, how long the rewards for being guilty are going to hold out.

On a merely practical plane, Dorothy Dinnerstein once again provides an explanation of how the status quo can actually seem the only choice. As she says, the attachment to this ongoing world helps make our awareness of our mortality painful. Our sense of personal significance is assaulted by the thought that this massive, vivid, human reality has managed before and will manage again to get on without us.

That is, things will take care of themselves. For many people in the past, this has been true. Unfortunately, as she and we must conclude, this sense is no longer supportable. To be victimized today is to be overdetermined. The environment, infant mortality, nuclear arsenals, human abuse, crack cocaine, illness, third-world starvation and exploitation, old-age penury, terrorism, slums, massive economic disparity between the middle class and the poor, and the third person singular wreak integrated havoc on more and more people. The noble calling simply will not do any longer, if it ever did.

The English tradition, however, has not been prone to acknowledge the equation between literacy and death, between the *Harbrace College Handbook* and malnutrition. Moreover, it seems to complicate matters to say that this is not merely a human issue or a global issue but a feminist issue whose chief feature is literacy education.

But this is what is to be said.

We live in an information economy. Our access to information determines our livelihoods, and the only access to information is through literacy. Of course, neither literacy nor feminism is uncomplicated, their relationship relatively unaddressed. On the one hand, literacy is a rather unique gatekeeper, an etiquette we bluff, an understanding we desecrate. On the other hand, it is too facile to simply assert that the cadre of subordinated female literacy instructors who for years have operated at the beck and call of others will shuck off the domination to change the face of literacy. Yet, in fact, if change is to occur — and the change will have to trample traditions of literacy just as it routs traditions of male dominance, then women are the ones who will have to change it. To be quite objective, if we assume that change in English teaching today will have to involve those who teach English today, then we must assume that the majority of people who are going to do the changing are white, middle-class women. Given the statistics for the participation of minority teachers in education in the future, the same applies.

The idea is enough to frighten every woman and man who is not white and to falsely calm numbers of men and women who are. The fright and falsity are, again, the point. The questions are: If we assume that those who know servitude can teach liberation, how will they do it? And if they can, why is literacy the agency? To put aside racial issues for the moment (on the assumption that gender prejudice precedes racial prejudice), the answers take two forms. Neither, on the face of it, seems promising.

The first answer is that nothing will come easy; solidarity among women will be hard. Simone de Beauvoir says that never in history have women constituted a group "set up *on its own account* against the male grouping" (80). Many women, in fact, enjoy privilege because they are subordinated. To reject subordination is to reject privilege. And that is an expensive proposition. De Beauvoir says, "as long as the temptations of convenience exist — in the economic inequality that favors certain individuals and the recognized right of woman to sell herself to one of these privileged men — she will need to make a greater moral effort than would a man in choosing the road of independence" (154). To put it another way, as Dinnerstein does, women have conformed to rules "at real inner cost"; their best achievement thus far may have been their fight to continue their own self-deception.

The second answer is that literacy is an instrument for change only because the power of literacy haunts every economic decision and action we take. It is inextricable from motive, yet it harrasses the methods of barter. The most trenchant argument put forward in this respect is by Gerda Lerner in *The Creation of Patriarchy*. Lerner sees literacy as the place where history and the subordination of women collide. Lerner's argument is long and complex, and literacy almost a peripheral element at times. But, literacy, she claims, is the first indicator of inequality: "If it were the case that the subordination of women antedated Western civilization, assuming civilization to have begun with the written historical record, my inquiry had to begin in the fourth millenium BC" (7). Pertaining explicitly to literacy, she says, "It is, of course, with the invention of writing and the keeping of written records that history begins" (57). She is claiming that literacy is itself primarily an instrument of domination. Whereas literacy itself is not necessarily some kind of mythic ruler, its interests have always reflected dominant interests, which were the interests of men.

Lerner may or may not be right about the beginnings of history. Her correlation of literacy with female subordination is invaluable, however. Literacy first documented property; primary property has always been women (an argument that Lerner says subsumes race and predates class). Literacy, therefore, is rooted in a system to exploit women.

Why, then, might we believe that women can change literacy? First, gender domination is different from all other forms. Women, no matter their race or class, enjoy a common history of second-class citizenship. True, it has not been the case that gender has ever bound women together, as every woman's movement thus far has shown. And, the exploitation and submission that middle-class white women have endured is partial and skewed. Other nonwhite, non-middle-class women have suffered far greater domination. Nonetheless, whereas it is imperative to recognize the double and triple subordination of many women, it is unnecessary to either patronize oppressed women or to make white women pay twice for their subordination (that which they have suffered and that which they haven't). What majority women and minority—basically economically secure versus economically tenuous and poor—women must recognize is that until all women share the articulation of domination, all women will be victims of centralized male power that forbids sharing. That is, women exist unskinned in the eyes of men; it is through their own efforts that women must peel away their race and class just along enough to recognize the domination that not merely turns them into victims but into victimizers who chiefly, if not cheerfully, work to maintain their own conditions of servitude. It is at that point when women can begin to reinvent the purpose and living of lives, and to realize that there is little need for women to see each other the way men have always seen them.

The second reason to believe that women—especially women who are literacy educators—can change the way things are is that they already have. The only tradition of revolutionary education in this country was promulgated by women. The women were neither free nor comfortable, but they undertook to educate the children scorned by the dominant society. They were the black women school teachers who taught prior to, during, and after Jim Crow and segregated education. The women knew black children were...children, and these women taught reading and writing long before white standardized tests said black students couldn't read or write. These were the women who endured miserable conditions because they knew misery was not a natural artifact of life, and these were the women who wrung from school years controlled by cotton, few or no textbooks, broken chairs and chalk boards, shoeless children—the only generations of educated black people there were. These were the women who were fired, ignored, retired, or harassed when desegregation came, their schools torn down, their constituency scattered. What greater evidence of the power and purpose of women who believe in education than that they be destroyed?

For, in fact, this women's movement in education, though it has never been called such and probably would not be by the women who marshalled it, was shut down. What these women attained was not enough to overcome the vitriol of racism or the subordination of gender. But what they set is an example, and what they suggest is the link between freedom and literacy. They did not lose because the link is weak but because the chain is strong. What they knew and what we must learn is that the chain itself must be broken in order that education, literacy, race, gender, and class no longer be contingent upon each other.

Perhaps this is what is meant by the feminization of literacy. Within a classroom informed by feminized literacy, teachers and students will learn to understand and to shed domination without having to trade one form of subordination for another. They will not do this without risk, and they will make mistakes. But they will not be alone.

In U.S. history there have been examples of feminized classrooms. Often these classrooms involved the collaboration of whites and blacks. The whites usually had corporate or missionary money; the blacks tithed most of what they had. During Reconstruction, white people, usually women funded by men, set up southern schools and colleges to educate blacks. During Jim Crow, blacks set up schools, including clandestine citizenship schools, to educate blacks, often aided and abetted by whites. Some white colleges, like Oberlin, refused to discriminate according to color or gender. Variously successfully, variously stable, these efforts lasted for a time.

The results are no fairy tales, however. Except according to the most generous measures, many efforts have slowly, painfully failed. Who in the late twentieth century can really laud the progress we have made when progress is measured by the cessation of lynching? In the current setting, why do we equate the skyrocketing number of school dropouts, grade-level repeaters, and those who eat free lunches with the color of children's skins or the rural poverty in which children live?

In the beginning of "Desire and Power: A Feminist Perspective," Catherine MacKinnon writes, "Sometimes, I think to myself, Mac-Kinnon, you write. Do you remember that the majority of the world's illiterates are women? *What are you doing?*" MacKinnon's point is well taken. But what she really means is that the women to whom and about whom she is writing will never hear her. For it is not first and foremost that the majority of the world's illiterates are women but that the majority of the world's women are exploited.

To write and to teach writing — to teach literacy — is to exercise a choice. Literacy is an idea with a violent history. We can continue that history or we can divert it. The signs are mostly discouraging. In a poem titled "From Sea to Shining Sea," June Jordan writes that our time is not a good time. It is not a good time, she says, to be gay, black, old, young, a woman or a child; not a good time to have a job, to be without a job, to have a gun or not to have a gun, to be against the natural order. In the last few stanzas she hesitates, however, and says. "Wait a minute." "This is a good time. This is the best time. This is the only time to come together."

She is at least right in one respect: it is certainly the only time. It is a bad time when literacy is used against poor people; it is a worse time when literacy educators use poor people to keep their jobs. How long and which educators continue to do this is a feminist issue. Whoever takes on the issue will take on the feminization of literacy.

Works Cited

de Beauvoir, Simone. *The Second Sex*. New York: Random House, Vantage, 1952.

Dinnerstein, Dorothy. *The Mermaid and the Minotaur: Sexual Arrangements and Human Malaise*. New York: Harper & Row, 1976.

Jordan, June. "From Sea to Shining Sea." *Home Girls: A Black Feminist Anthology*. Ed. Barbara Smith. New York: Kitchen Table/Women of Color Press, 1983. 223–29.

Lerner, Gerda. *The Creation of Patriarchy*. New York: Oxford UP, 1986.

MacKinnon, Catherine A. "Desire and Power: A Feminist Perspective." *Marxism and Culture*. Eds. Cary Nelson and Lawrence Grossberg. Chicago: U of Illinois P, 1988. 105–12.

Smith, Barbara, ed. Introduction. *Home Girls: A Black Feminist Anthology*. New York: Kitchen Table/Women of Color Press, 1983. xxiv.

Rodríguez Milanés: I think the function of education is to put designs on us, and that causes resistance, and that leads to growth, or retrogression, I don't know. The students resist me, first as being Latina, as being young, having more power than they do, and working-class, that I didn't have a car, and I didn't go to camp, and I didn't have a ranch house with split level and garage, and, you know, the two or three others in the classroom that are like me, that came from an urban area, that were working-class and maybe didn't speak— well for sure didn't speak standard English at home—are amazed at the power and how at ease and just how comfortable [the other] students are. And this afternoon, I was telling Mark and Michael that when I turn the tables and say, "Well, I'm going to share the authority with you because I am not comfortable with authority," they seem to accept it just immediately.

Berlin: Right!

Rodríguez Milanés: No problem, fine! You know? [laughter] And then I have to take back and say, "Wait a minute! I like my authority, let me have some more of it!" You know?

Berlin: Yeah.

Rodríguez Milanés: So, I'm not...I don't think there's a problem with the word *resistance*. If there wasn't any resistance to me, I'd be worried.

12

Risks, Resistance, and Rewards
One Teacher's Story

Cecilia Rodríguez Milanés

Resistance to feminist pedagogy, political/social concerns in the composition/literature classroom, and to myself, a young Latina instructor, has been something I've come to expect from my students. After all, most of them are white, middle-class, young men and women who enter college courses convinced that racism and sexism are issues from the sixties that have no place in "English."[1] Students who feel uncomfortable, or even annoyed, that their literature/composition classroom is no longer a place safe from the "world" need to be reassured that their anger is legitimate. I express my anger that social issues were hidden from me as an English student learning to read in the New Critical way. It is extremely important to me that those students who believe that some of us are overzealous readers feel safe in expressing their disagreement and dismay. Resistance may exert itself in blocking the class's collaborative/cooperative process; others resist through silence. Perhaps it is perverse to say it, but I have found myself looking forward to student resistance; it means that they are alive, awake. Resistance keeps me honest and on my toes—trying to find ways of usefully redirecting students' anger. Resistance teaches me; it leads to negotiation, communication. Negotiation in this alternative classroom attempts to avoid the confrontational, argumentative nature of debate in the traditional phallocentric view.

For me, cooperation and collaboration between teachers and students, students and students, are essential in providing an atmosphere of trust and respect. One of the problems of using resistance as a heuristic is that friction between teachers and students, students and students, is inevitable. I combat this by emphasizing the classroom as a community: a place where people have to live and work together—at least for a semester. In the community of my classroom, decisions are agreed upon by consensus; texts are chosen by election; students' texts are shared and read aloud, and grades are earned by completing the terms of a teacher/student-authored contract. Yet, even as I write these words I betray myself, a writer, whose business it is to tell stories. I'll tell stories here about how all decisions could not be made by consensus, how I chose most of the texts, how my presence as the teacher—just as democratic and equalitarian as I fancied myself to be—manipulated the contract. Perhaps it is appropriate to fess up right at the beginning of this story. After all, part of the function of the English classroom, as I see it, is to provide students with the opportunity of seeing themselves as writers and readers of the world, not just texts. In order to achieve this, or even approach this, I tend to take a lot of risks in the classroom. I take chances, all in the hopes of forming a community where students' stories and readings may find voice. By risk taking, I rewrite the traditional competitive classroom; the resistance that results becomes a way of learning for us all.

In telling my story, I embrace the anti-patriarchal, nontraditional dimensions of narrative, the form closest to my heart. The story begins with my return to the composition/literature classroom after being on loan one semester to the Women's Studies department, co-facilitating an Introduction to Feminism course. I will move between the Fall and Spring semesters of one school year, between two sections of a course entitled Reading Prose Fiction. I will give voice here to my students' evaluations, comments, and responses to the classes and me. This way I'll provide more context and "dialog" to this story of how I sought to foster a dialogic pedagogy.

Okay, so here I was walking to my first class, enjoying the crisp fall air ushering me along, a vision of the Introduction to Feminism course still shining in my head. Images of students dealing with the most pressing issues of the day—imperialism, classism, racism, sexism, all those isms. How could Reading Prose Fiction compete with such exciting stuff? The Intro to Feminism students were immersed in feminist pedagogy/process; they were engaged students, active, questioning. Could I recast the English class to resemble the Women's Studies course? I walked into that cramped, narrow classroom (in the basement of a dorm building, no less) and saw lots of white male faces; furrowed brows shielded eyes that scrutinized me, or the board behind me. The long rows of desks stuffed with visibly uncomfortable bodies scared the hell out of me. Did I really want to be in English? In retrospect, I suppose I was trying to decide. I told them my story: I'm a graduate student in the English doctoral program. I am not into authority but by virtue of the fact that I've been assigned to "teach" this course I have the authority to do whatever I want—we peon grad students have a tremendous amount of freedom here to learn about our own teaching. This whole semester will be a running experiment; you all are the guinea pigs (talk about authority). I want to make this class democratic; I want to facilitate instead of "professing," give voice to everyone (by use of rotating chair) instead of choosing the same students over and over, I want to practice feminist/political pedagogy. I want you to look at each other, move into a circle, know each other's names. Those blank faces just kept staring. It didn't occur to me then to ask them what they wanted from the class, and while I don't recall any rolling eyes, I imagine there were some—probably some muttered curses too. When I tell them my story and what I hope for them, it doesn't all sink in at the beginning but what becomes apparent is that I want to deal with them fairly, that I want to hear their voices, and that we have a great deal to talk/write about.

One day later that semester, I asked the class to divide themselves into small discussion groups. I audiotaped one group to see if the students would follow directed questions in their discussion. Since the room was so small and the acoustics were so bad, half of the groups met in an empty adjacent room. I flitted between the groups and rooms. At the end of the class hour, everyone returned to the main room, and one of the young men, the only other Latino, picked up the tape recorder and talked into it while I was turned away. He was surrounded by a group of young men. There was lots of talk going on because we were getting ready to adjourn for the day. I remember seeing him there with the machine in his hand and wondered what message he had for me. What I heard that night after I rewound the tape was plenty to think about: "This teacher is a feminist and her views are fucked up."

I was duly shocked, chagrined, and all that. Then I had to deal with it. I played his message over only once or twice because I didn't want to get too angry; I was angry enough. Dealing with it meant asking the student to stay after class the next time. My heart was pounding in my chest when I approached him; the students around him gave him and each other looks—they must have known. After everyone had gone, before I could say anything to him, he apologized and said he had written me a note and was trying to deliver it to me the day "it" happened but couldn't find me. At first he was polite, awkwardly so, but the longer he talked—I just let him talk—the more ardent he got. He said that he had had his "share of feminist teachers" and that he didn't think this was going to be a productive class for him if I was going to push my ideas on him. I asked him why and how he thought I was pushing my ideas on him. He blamed the reading list; of the first five stories, four were by women. The stories I selected were "loaded" texts, texts that lent themselves to political readings, such as Mary E. Wilkins Freeman's "The Revolt of 'Mother'" and Charlotte Perkins Gilman's "The Yellow Wallpaper." After unburdening himself of the injustices he felt he'd suffered (I had put him in an uncomfortable position, implying the guilt by association syndrome—him being a male and therefore oppressor), he volunteered that he was speaking for the "other guys" in the class. I remembered the group of young men around him, their chuckles in the background of the tape. I thanked him for his honesty and told him, honestly, that I was annoyed by his message to me on the tape, that I found it rude, but that I was glad we could clear the air. That was all I had planned to say; he actually had done most of the talking up until then. I had wild ideas about him dropping the class or, oh horror, a scene with him screaming at me in front of the class. But this was too easy—I mean all I had to do was listen? After that conversation, this student felt comfortable enough with me to seek me out for advice and help in choosing future English courses or just to talk.

In trying to move away from the traditional, competitive, patriarchal classroom, I rewrote, little by little (this was very risky for me) what constituted my authority (of course, the teacher's authority can never be completely undermined, the university sees to that). In the first section, I had drawn up a grading contract that emphasized work quantity over graded assignments. I wanted to see if they would do all the work, even the required revisions, and honor the contract, thereby relieving me of what I have come to believe is an idiosyncratic exercise—grading students' texts (we had had a long discussion in the beginning of the term about the nature and function of grading). I was afraid the students would blow off the requirements, hand in the minimum, do the least.[2] In both sections, with the exception of one or two students (never the same ones), backsliding was not an issue. The contracts stipulated that attendance was crucial, and I found that, again with two exceptions in each term, attendance was regular and consistent. In the beginning of both semesters, the students really didn't believe the contract, that is, they couldn't understand why there were no grades on their papers. After the first few weeks and papers, the dismayed looks disappeared and, while understanding an alternative epistemology may not have required their agreement with its tenents, these students slipped into accepting it as the way things were for the class and seemed to enjoy the class and our discussions. My compensation included vital, critical, and many times, loud discussions of issues ranging from ethnocentrism, nuclear proliferation, and sexual double standards to arguments for and against candidates. Almost universally, they wrote more than the minimum; their work was usually quite reflective and thoughtful. And while the students overwhelmingly preferred the contracts, there was resistance to the contract too, but I'll save those stories for later.

Drew: I thought the basic idea was very good and has a lot of potential. When the student is relieved from the pressure of having to perform for grades, he/she is free to work unhindered by what the professor may think of his/her work. The problem is that some students may not take the work seriously. However, the benefit outweighs the detractions.

Cary: I thought the course was set up to produce quantity, not *necessarily* quality in our assignments.

Eileen: I'm pleased with the way this class is structured. Truthfully, I was proud of myself for having worked hard on the revisions. At first I thought that I wouldn't have to do a lot of work since the paper wasn't being graded—but I couldn't feel good about myself handing in a paper that I didn't put a lot of effort into.

My status as a young feminist Latina graduate instructor worked both for and against me in the classroom. I spoke the students' language (informal, vernacular, nonacademic) and moved easily between the roles of teacher and student and writer and reader. I became a class member, albeit with more power than other class members. Sometimes I had no power, especially when it came to responding to students' texts. Because they had writing groups all semester and were not graded on their work, my comments to them sometimes went unacknowledged. In the second semester I paid particular attention and spent considerable time in reading and responding to the students' papers. In striving for the kind of facilitative commentary that Knoblauch and Brannon discuss in *Rhetorical Traditions and the Teaching of Writing*, I sought to problematize and engage students' ideas, not usurp them. After putting so much energy into responding to students' texts, it was frustrating when my comments went unacknowledged. I directly asked them to respond to my comments, but with every batch of papers there would be student memos ignoring my concerns in the memo. I decided that most of their silences in response to my annotations meant that they simply didn't agree with me. I had to learn to accept that; after all, the contract I cowrote stipulated that as long as they did their drafts and revisions, they would be complying. I had authorized their resistance to my comments and could not *force* my readings, of any texts, on them.

An instance where my status as a Latina specifically worked against me concerns the reading list. Many students attributed the "slant" of the reading list to my ethnicity and gender (although if they had analyzed the list they would have seen that it was gender- and race-balanced). I used most of the same short texts both semesters, changing the novels for the second class—two of the three novels we used were chosen by the students. I strove for a broad range and representation of short fiction, yet sometimes students expressed dissatisfaction with my selections. Below are some of their comments, but first a story about resistance to Latin American fiction (and perhaps the question of ethnicity).

Magic realism, or the "marvelous real" as Latin Americans call it, can be off-putting for readers unaccustomed to it. I suspected that reading the likes of Márquez, Borges, Valenzuela, et al. would be daunting for many of the students early in the semester, so I moved that reading toward the end of the term. I knew from past classes that most of the students would love Woody Allen's story "The Kugelmass Episode," about a middle-class New Yorker who gets a magician to send him into texts such as *Madame Bovary* so that he could have affairs. I made sure that we read this story, with its references to well-known spots in New York City and the kind of dialog students easily related to, before we got anywhere near the Latin Americans. When we finally read Márquez's "Very Old Man with Enormous Wings," some students expressed dislike. It was a gorgeous Spring day and we met outside in the courtyard surrounded by daffodils. One student spoke to the circle: "It's stupid. There's no such thing as angels." Another volunteered, "Maybe it lost something in the translation." This last comment gnawed at me, despite the sunshine and soft grass, because a few students used it over and over in expressing their disinterest and dissatisfaction with the texts by Latin American writers. I wondered out loud why they had no problems believing a story about a magic box in New York City. They sort of shrugged their shoulders and so did I. Perhaps I should have persisted in getting an answer, but then again, I suspect we were all infected with Spring fever and the whimsy and humor of Márquez allowed us to leave the question hanging on the warm breeze.

Brad: I feel there were too many Cuban fantasy writers. Remembering how most people reacted to these stories I think this may be the general consensus of the class. I know personally that these stories were not appreciated in the context that they may be understood in other cultures. Once explained in class these stories took on a more reasonable acceptance. Except for these exceptions I raised before, I feel the reading list was a fine spectrum of literature.

Rick: There was *way* too much emphasis on minorities and feminism. I felt that feminism was read into everything I wrote. But, as a whole I would highly recommend this class to anyone who asked.

Betty: I think you impose your feelings about feminism on the class. Often times I don't agree with what you call [chauvinism]. We could read a story about electricity and you would read in chauvanism. I think overzealous judgment undermines and lessens the feminist movement for equality.

Annette: I find one thing to bother me and that is that we concentrate too much on predjudice issues. I become depressed and a little annoyed after reading such pieces of work.

Ben: The second page [of the reading list] is where I see the problem. The stories tend to be of Cuban and Spanish origin, or else of feminist appeal. I respect the fact that you're proud of your heritage and sex, but there appeared to be an overdose here.

What's noteworthy about these comments is the students' reactions to noncanonical texts and their specific mention of Cuban writers. In the first term we read two Cuban writers — Lydia Cabrera, a folklorist, and novelist Reinaldo Arenas — neither of which I would call "fantasy" writers; in the second term we read only a short piece by Cabrera. It is also interesting to see how easily and unself-consciously they responded to my request. After all, I had asked them for their opinion of the reading list, and no other English professor had so earnestly done that before.

Though the first semester was a decidedly more resistant group, the community atmosphere of the class played down hostility and encouraged them to give me and each other the benefit of the doubt. My approach showed a sincerity of wanting to understand them, their ideas, disagreements and their anger. My greatest task was in finding ways to redirect anger into useful, not hurtful, articulation. We didn't all end up agreeing with each other, but we, at the very least, tolerated and respected each other.

The last two stories are about authority and the contract; the first one happened in the Fall, when I brought to the class's attention that two students had not turned in their papers but that one had contacted me and still wanted an A. This student had seen me three days before the paper was due and informed me that the draft and all the notes were in a textbook that was stolen. We talked about it and I told her to go ahead and rewrite it and to get it to me as soon as she could. I then decided to take it to the class, thinking that I was escaping some of my authority. I approached the front of the room — that's where the board always is, isn't it — and asked the class to vote on one of the options I had come up with or to suggest another: (1) Accept the student's paper late and have him/her write an extra one, (2) Accept the student's paper late but reduce his/her final grade, or (3) Accept the student's paper late but have him/her read and comment on everyone's paper.

No one questioned that I had generated the options and predetermined that I would indeed take a late paper. They simply accepted them as the only alternatives; they just went ahead and voted. The votes were tallied and the young woman accepted her fate and wrote another paper. The usual shuffling of feet and scratching of desks across the cheap linoleum filled the room with atmosphere as we got ready to start the day's discussion. One young woman asked me about the other student, the other paper that wasn't turned in. I told her that the student had not approached me as yet. She said, "Well, I wouldn't either; that's too intimidating." I said, "But am I intimidating?" (friendly class "member" that I imagined myself to be). She said, "Well, yes. Not as much, but you're still the teacher. You give the grade." There was a pause and then, nodding my head, I said, "You're absolutely right. I am still the teacher." So authority, no matter how hard I tried to obscure it, manifested itself. I always think of John Cougar Mellencamp's song that goes something like, I fight authority; authority always wins.

The other story is about the second section, about two-thirds into the term. This class was an easier group because, proportionately, there was an equal number of men and women. However, there were about a half dozen students that liked to chat with each other but not with the whole circle. They tended to congregate near the door for an easy exit. One or two of them would get to class early enough to save seats for the others, so there was always a quorum of them at all times. It was only during writing groups that they were split up because I insisted on them forming groups with people from opposite sides of the circle. Every couple of days I would interrupt their private conversations and call attention to their rudeness, noting that other class members had listened to their input during the discussion. Anyway, on this particular day, as the rest of the class moved the desks into a circle, a few students gathered around me to hand in late papers or incomplete assignments. These few, their faces displaying grave concern, wanted to give me excuses before turning their papers in. As a class we had come to consensus on what were legitimate excuses, and what I was hearing didn't sound like any of those. I asked these students to see me after class, but I was bothered. Hadn't the contract, the one we wrote together, clearly outlined the guidelines and due dates for papers? I was antsy about getting to work, and so I asked someone to begin the discussion with a go-around, where everyone in the circle speaks to a sentence/passage or whatever. The half dozen conversationalists were having a grand old time on one side of the room, and then one young woman from the other side flippantly said, "Start with me—I didn't read it so go on to the next person." There were chuckles and then a lull—even the talkers' attention was seized. Here it was, I thought, they're testing me.

Somehow, the people who had crowded around me with late papers and lame excuses, the disregard for the contract (which stipulated that all reading was required before coming to class), the chattering, the smirks — it all came to a head and I felt compelled to talk *at* the class. . . . Okay, so I yelled at them. There. I shocked myself. I took out a copy of the contract, waved it at them, and reread out loud some of the requirements, reminding them that they had authored this contract. I asked them why they had put me into this position, this position of authority (my neck veins were bulging by then). I told them again that I didn't like that position and that I was trying to be democratic not authoritarian. I was angry, and after about five minutes of scolding them for not being more responsible, I shut my mouth. Guilt began to pulse at my temples. There was silence. I like to think that some of them hung their heads in shame, for that was exactly what I was doing. After some awkward moments and nervous coughing, one of the students began the discussion, the work of the day. Others joined in, circling around for different readings/responses to the text. When class was over, I still felt so badly that I asked some of the students who stayed after what they thought of it all. Most of these congratulated me, saying they were glad I had said those things and that I should have done it long ago. I wasn't convinced, especially since some of these were the very ones who had late papers. I had to talk to someone else about it and sought out a good friend and told her. She helped me to see that I had expressed my honest feeling to them, and that it would have been anti-feminist to repress that anger. She reminded me that all I had said was that I wasn't happy about the position they had put me in, that of pedant.

So I yelled. They yelled at each other from time to time when discussing something or other, but I found that in both classes tolerance reigned. That is not to say that hostility never reared its ugly head, but when it did, we talked it out, talked around it, negotiated the disagreement at hand, and moved past it. Before, students had understood negotiation to mean an adherence to argument and debate, but in my classes, negotiation was never one person winning at the expense of another; that would be exclusionary and anti-feminist. Through collaboration in writing groups, cooperation and collective activity (such as coming to consensus on issues related to the contract), students began to retreat from the combative, patriarchal forms of learning. Providing this kind of space in the classroom allowed my students the freedom to tell me when and where and how they thought I was wrong. I had authorized their resistance, and I like it that way. Telling you these stories about the risks I took and the resistance I encountered, I recognize my own resistance to this alternative pedagogy. But as I said before, I've come to understand resistance as a form of learning for me and for my students, and that's reward enough.

Notes

1. Twelve percent of the student population at SUNYA are made up of blacks and Latinos, 2 percent are foreign students, the rest are white — which may explain some of the resistance I faced.

2. This is a portion of the contract cowritten by myself and the students in the Spring section of Reading Prose Fiction:

> *For the grade of A:*
>
> I. Full and active participation in large- and small-group discussions and writing groups
> II. Two 3–5 p. typed papers, with all revisions to be handed in on time. Copies of drafts I and II of both papers required for each writing group member.
> III. No more than 3 unexcused absences; each tardy of more than 10 mins. will equal a quarter (1/4) absence.
> IV. Journal entries of a minimum one half p. for each story; 4 entries for each novel (2 pp.). Students may miss 3 entries from the total number.
> V. Three essays to be written in class. Dates will be announced ahead of time and any persons missing these must have a valid excuse and must make up the essay within one week of the original date.

For the grades of B and C, students were entitled to more absences and fewer journal entries. Revisions and participation in writing and discussion groups were still required, but students were not required to do all of the in-class essays. The requirements for grades of D or less reflected what the class believed to be excessive absences and a noncommitted student — someone who wasn't active in groups, seldom revised, or was inconsistent in keeping a journal.

Knoblauch: And you can make them uncomfortable in flashes. I mean they know, they know the liberal rituals of conversation and will engage in them, but they also understand that there's a lot at stake if those images and moral lessons are truly subverted. It you get to that point, where they're starting to puzzle about those conditions, you can, you can watch them back off. It's just too jeopardizing for them. Then you have to ask yourself as a teacher what the next step is. Do you then take the next step [laughs] and what kind of chaos—is it, at that point, a constructive chaos that you've got in the classroom? I don't know whether it is or not, and so far that's where I've stopped, and you may wonder where your responsibility really lies at that point, when you know you've got people at just that edge of radical insecurity. I mean, with the Bambara story, it's a classic liberal response and a classic conservative response. The conservative response is, if they work harder they'll get there. The liberal response is, everybody ought to be able to buy thousand-dollar toy sailboats. Those are comfortable because they're within the realm of the experience that these folks have. We start challenging FAO Schwartz as a cultural sign, and they begin to realize what's at stake for them in that challenge, and then you get real resistance, I mean, talk about *resistance*—

North: Surely, then, you're bluffing—even more. You drive to work in your car—

Knoblauch: Yessss.

North: I mean, that becomes such an obvious bluff. Maybe that's the reason nobody wants to take the next step—

Berlin: What—'cause none of us can afford thousand-dollar sailboats? What're you talking aobut? Come on, none of us even desires—see the thing that bothers me is that their notions of what the good life is are divided along these lines. Either you don't make it or you make it so well, I mean, come on. What kind of range of response to your experience do they have—do *we* have when those are the alternatives: either I can buy everything or I can buy nothing. You know, come on.

Knoblauch: In the meantime, their images of poverty are vicarious, for the most part. They're not real images at all until you—I don't know how to make them real, you know, it—mass media—does such a good job of erasing images of poverty.

Berlin: Yeah, that's right.

Knoblauch: And these kids are just *fed* on mass media images. And it's real tough to get through that—

Harris: Cy, in your story, you had the, you used the phrase—I don't know if necessarily you want to stick with it—I mean that, you had sort of brought them to the brink of an insecurity, and I don't think that's quite the right phrase. I mean, it seems to me that what you've done is made a certain insecurity that's already there more apparent. And as pitiful and outrageous the system of exploitation that this country runs on is, I don't think that's the pitch I would want to make to my students. Rather, I think I would want to make something more like Jim's [Berlin's] pitch, except just perhaps in less absolute terms.

That is to say, the image of the good life that is offered our students has to be bought at considerable psychic cost. I think we'd agree, at least in part, to refuse elements of that purchase, to say [to students], "It's not, not going to work."

Knoblauch: Right—

Harris: I think that certain images of the good life are fraudulent...and that we can talk to upper-middle-class white male students about the fraudulence of the good life that is set up with them, for them. And that's where I would want to make my pitch more than saying—I know this is a horrible reduction—but, you know, "Don't you feel socially guilty about who you're stepping on?" There's a way in which I think we can appeal to them on this more selfish level, and I think this is part of what Steve's concerns are—that we have, in fact, organized our own lives fairly selfishly.

13

Rhetoric, Responsibility, and the "Language of the Left"

Stephen M. North

The "prospectus" for this volume, our invitation to participate, proposed, among other things, that those of us involved in it would "publicly engage and examine our own developing processes of self-scrutiny and resistance in order to investigate, together, the educational and ideological assumptions that they enact and the positive educational developments that they promote" (1). So far, so good. With a momentary pause over *resistance*—the reasons for which I'll explain in a moment—this was a proposal I could live with, especially since the proposed investigation really would be public and collaborative, with circulated drafts, roundtable discussions, and revisions. I figured to learn a lot and, as it turns out, I have. However, that wasn't the end of what the prospectus proposed: "we begin," the editors said a little further on, "by attempting to determine what we mean when we use terms like 'critical consciousness,' 'ideology,' 'liberation' and 'resistance'" (4).

Here was a complication. My reaction—and this accounts for that pause over *resistance*—was that these were terms I really *don't* use. I don't mean that I haven't heard or read them, or haven't talked with people who used them. Teaching where I teach, reading what I read, I'd have been hard-pressed not to have become aware over the past several years that more and more people in composition studies have come to use terms like these, featuring them in rhetoric that, given the prevailing valence of the field's traditional discourses, can be described as deliberately provocative, "ideologically charged": in reaction to the generally perceived center-to-right tendencies of that tradition, most of this has been rhetoric from the political left, deriving much of its power from resonances in Marxist thought. My own points of contact — the easily documentable ones, anyway — are probably not unusual: reading Paulo Freire, for example (having been led to him by Ann Berthoff); being on the mailing list for the newsletter of the Progressive Composition Caucus; serving on a CCCC panel with Patricia Bizzell, Bruce Herzberg, and Cy Knoblauch on "Writing against the Curriculum," which focused pretty heavily on concepts like critical teaching and resistance, and so on.

And yet despite my awareness that such terms are characteristic of some of the composition community's various discourses, they do not represent the language in which I characteristically speak or write or think. Not in the way I don't speak, write, or think in Chinese, say, or in the argot of contemporary physics. In those discourses, too many sounds and symbols are simply mysteries. In this case, there are few mysteries in that sense; and, in fact, I can even demonstrate a passable fluency. I composed the following statement as a kind of test run:

> As a college professor of English, I am committed to a personally and politically liberatory pedagogy. I aim to foster in my students a critical consciousness that will make them aware of their situation within a late 20th-century capitalist state — a process by which they may well discover themselves to be victims of that state's insidious forms of class oppression. In doing so, I hope to empower all of them to resist the forces exerted upon them, and to help at least some of them to reinterpret their current oppositional behaviors — unreflective and isolated acts of defiance — as symptomatic of an inchoate anger over the acts of exclusion that are responsible for their marginalization, and so lead them toward the self-reflection and collectivity that are the hallmarks of true resistance.

Granted, full-fledged statements on teaching aren't very common outside of tenure review dossiers (where they tend to be more guardedly, not to say cynically, cast), so that this sub-genre may have some parodic side effects. But I've tried this passage out on a variety of readers, and though a few of them have sensed parody or caricature — especially, perhaps, since I was asking whether the passage was guilty of either — they couldn't say where or why, exactly. Still, my ability to concoct plausible statements using such language is really beside the point. Even though plenty of people I respect describe their work in terms like these, and even though there are ways in which it might be a desirable thing for me to demonstrate our "solidarity" by adopting it, too, I really can't — or, at any rate, and for what the distinction is worth, I can't and *mean* it, and so I won't. In the rest of this essay, I will try to explain why.

In view of the project this volume represents, the logical place for me to begin is by saying that I can't — won't — use this language to describe my teaching. This is hardly a new issue. Some years ago, for instance, Peter Elbow approached essentially the same problem in "The Pedagogy of the Bamboozled," in which—as the title hints—he asks how the major principles of Freire's *The Pedagogy of the Oppressed* relate to his situation: that of "a teacher hired by an educational *institution* to teach mostly non-adult, middle-class students" (87, his emphasis). Elbow reiterates those major principles. First, the teacher must work as a collaborating ally of the students, not a supervisor. Second, the subject of study must be the students' perceptions of their own lives, always to be problematized. Third, the goal of study is to change not only the students but the world itself—"external, objective reality" (90). And fourth, the process must be primarily rational and cognitive, featuring critical thinking, problem posing, and so on.

I think that's a pretty fair representation of Freire's position; and, in a restricted sense, I am quite satisfied with Elbow's framing of the dilemma that these principles present:

> My argument can be summarized as follows. Freire gives principles which I think very few institutional teachers in this country follow. But I think many teachers, both in high school and in college, *imply* in subtle ways that they do follow these principles. In this way, they bamboozle students and themselves. Thus there are two possible reforms: start really doing what Freire describes; or stop implying that you do. (87)

Given this analysis, I would, like Elbow, have to opt for the second choice. This semester, for example, I am teaching Tutoring and Writing (a course preparing undergraduates to work in our Writing Center) and Composition Theory (a graduate introduction to the field of composition). In terms of the first principle, then, however collaborative I think my teaching practices are (not to mention how my students perceive them), I am contracted—to the university, through tuition to the students, and in both senses quite consciously—as the supervisor: the grader, the sorter, the ranker. In terms of the second principle, both courses begin with autobiographical writings, and we return often to their experiences as teachers and tutors, writers and readers. Still, however relevant the courses might be to my students' lives (and again, their views surely are crucial), I don't think I could say those lives are the courses' central concern. The third principle I'll frame as a question: Will the teaching/learning in these courses change the world? Well, as I've suggested, most of my students are or soon will be tutors and teachers, so in that sense our time together might have a transformative effect, in some cases right away. But that would be true, so far as I can see, whatever my ideological claims. I'm pretty sure this isn't quite the "praxis" Freire has in mind. At any rate, as any number of commentators have pointed out, it isn't clear how a notion of "praxis" worked out among Brazilian peasants can transfer to an American, state-funded research university. And for the last principle: Does this learning/teaching highlight reason and cognition—in particular, the deploying of something Freire might acknowledge to be critical consciousness? I'm not sure. In both courses, it might be fairer to say I feature rationality to make my students suspicious of authoritative claims, including reasoned ones, in various contexts. In this sense, if they "learn" what I try to "teach," see what I try to reveal, I think they have a chance to exercise power, create a space in which to speak: in Freire's term, to name the world, or at least those parts of it we're working in. But separated from the other three principles, I think I'd be guilty of "bamboozling" were I to claim Freire's imprimatur for this one.

Still, it is not only, or even mostly, the failure of this language to describe my teaching that explains my inability to adopt it. I am always struck, even here in Elbow's essay, by our willingness to circumscribe our discussion of such matters within the boundaries of our classrooms or, in our more expansive moods, our "professional lives." In his Preface to the 1987 edition of *Critical Teaching and Everyday Life*, Ira Shor suggests that for "liberatory learning to help in remaking society, we can consider being more than the very best critical teachers every day in our classrooms. We can also try to be the very best teachers and citizens outside of the school, in the community, the profession, the society at large; in groups, movements, and political arenas which influence social policy" (xiii). I was surprised to see this—not because I disagree with Shor's reasoning, which makes sense to me, but because I rather thought it would have been a given, would have gone *without* saying. In fact, I remain surprised by the gentleness of his position. We can "consider" pursuing this way of being outside of the classroom? Consider? I don't get it. Can you imagine him actually saying the opposite: Remember, critical teaching and liberatory learning are strictly nine-to-five, classroom notions. When you're not with your students, practice political indifference; grab for everything you can get; support oppression.

I don't want to oversimplify the difficulties involved here. In a terrific essay in *College English*, John Clifford, responding to James Merod's *The Political Responsibility of the Critic*, explains his reservations about what he characterizes as Merod's call for "changes in consciousness and institutional structure" (523). The former, Clifford suggests, though enormously difficult, might be possible; but he is, with Kenneth Burke and Frank Lentricchia, "less sanguine" about the latter, "about the efficacy of overt political action" (523). Following Lentricchia, he suggests that we can be most politically valuable doing what we do best, whether that is teaching writing or interpreting contemporary fiction. This is the Gramscian notion of specific intellectuals working for transformation at the site they find themselves. It seems difficult enough trying to modify a traditional curriculum without dissipating one's energy at the barricades. Trying to empower students to read critically without repressing their own cultural values and beliefs, trying to persuade colleagues that the worldly perspective of a critical pedagogy can enrich their teaching — these are awesome tasks that one can spend a career trying to achieve without great success. Do we need, can we afford, the frustrations of failing to make a dent in Third World literacy or the drop-out rate of urban high schools? I hope my focusing is not a flight from political responsibility, but rather a modest deployment of finite emotional and intellectual resources, a nonutopian attempt to raise the consciousness of a few to the racism, sexism, and political manipulation that can be found in the texts of all cultures. (523)

What's at issue is not, Clifford concludes, "a question of goals," but of "tactics." "Intellectual manifestos like [Merod's] can create the professional solidarity needed to enact change, but it is only our daily struggles to empower students that can create the emotional force needed for a transformational praxis" (523).

As I said above, people I respect — and John Clifford is definitely one of them — describe their work in terms of the language in question, and I understand the dilemma he presents and provisionally resolves in that language. But I confess I also find myself puzzled by that resolution. When I try to use it to account for my own way of life — try, that is, to share his "hope" that, in the terms offered by this language, the "focusing" he offers "is not a flight from political responsibility" — I feel very uncomfortable. In an average academic week, I am in a classroom for maybe six hours. Say I spend another fifteen on preparation, mostly reading student writing. Another six or eight is invested in formal meetings — in contact, that is, with colleagues. That's fewer than thirty hours each week given directly to what John characterizes as "awesome tasks." But even if I tinkered with the figures to produce a forty- or fifty-hour week, that would still leave a good seventy waking hours per week during the thirty-week academic year to account for, not to mention all those hours in the twenty-two weeks classes are not in session.

I know where those hours currently go: to three kids in three schools; to their dog, schoolwork, religious education, piano lessons, Girl Scouts, swimming, gymnastics, soccer; to writing like this, and its attendant reading; to parents (now also grandparents), brothers and sisters, cousins and friends; to mowing the lawn, cooking meals, washing clothes and dishes, shoveling the driveway, and all such household duties; to taxes and landlording, mortgages, insurance, auto repair; to running, golf, basketball, or whatever other games are available. In short, they are spent in or on a life that I would characterize as a system-supporting, system-supported, pro-capitalist, American mainstream life. It is a life that, so far as I can tell, I would fight to defend—or at least one that, in the face of a fair number of genuine options, I keep on living. Were I to shift over, though, commit myself to the language of critical teaching—of liberatory learning, of a socially revolutionary pedagogy were I to enlist to fight in what Shor has described as the "vast arena of culture war called education" ("Educating" 26) I would feel compelled to change that life, as well.

So while I appreciate the intent of this Gramscian notion concerning the role of intellectuals in such a struggle, I think that, at least in my case, it would come very quickly to feel like a dubious dispensation, and not one I could live with. Far from seeing action at the barricades as "dissipating one's energy," I would expect it to be—even more than Shor's "consider" implies—an essential feature of such a life, and positive, energizing. Yes, my intellectual and emotional resources are finite, need careful marshalling; that's the case even now. But in a life conceived in terms of Shor's "culture war," a life wherein I acknowledged that others, whatever the finitude of *their* resources, could afford to be "at the barricades," I don't see how I could reconcile forty- or fifty- or sixty-hour weeks of even the most concentrated academic consciousness-raising with either a politically unchallenged institution or a way of life that, for the other 128 (or 118 or 108) hours of each week, denied or ignored or otherwise discounted that conception and acknowledgement—or the urgency of both.

So you might say—I might say—that I cannot commit myself to this language because it not only fails to describe my teaching but because, in a more profound way, it fails to accord with the rest of my life: whatever I might do in the classroom, this language of critical teaching and liberatory learning would seem to commit me to ideas and, more especially, to actions to which I am, outside of that classroom, simply not committed.

And, in fact, I do say that, but I want to go farther. All discourses, I think, can be said to have rules for dealing with what might be called—in this case, with a particularly obvious aptness—resistance. To adapt the analysis offered by Joseph Harris and Jay Rosen in "Teaching Writing as Cultural Criticism" (their contribution to this volume), the discourses we encounter can be said to try, in their various ways, to "position" us. And in large part the power for such positioning—as in this sentence, for example, where I'm stuck responding to the convention of treating discourses as Their Royal,

Sentient, Always-Alreadynesses, however much I might drag my feet—is a function of the penalties levied for discursive noncompliance. Precisely how this works—what it is that makes us accept the conventions of some discourses and resist others; or, to stay with Their Always-Alreadynesses, what it is that determines how we come to position and reposition ourselves, or to be positioned and repositioned by them, as they conflict in constituting us—all that is what, albeit it in a limited way, I'm trying to figure out in this essay.

To that end, I want to return to the passage I quoted from John Clifford. Clearly, I cannot speak for John (although I am speaking to him). I chose the passage because it is as close as I have seen anyone come to accounting in this language for the way I would account for my teaching and living. However, as I hope I have made clear, it is *not* an account I can accept. When I try it on, try to say it for or about myself, it just doesn't work. It comes out as a feeble, guilt-ridden, handwringing apology: "The Struggle is so vast, and I am so weak and self-indulgent and phony, full of false dreams and wrongheaded loyalties! What a sham!" This unhappy sensation is, I would argue, the result of resistance: it delineates the posture ("Assume the position!") forced upon those who, in this case, try to speak honestly from the far right of the Left, if you will. And it ain't pretty.

Now, maybe all this seems, despite my insistence to the contrary, like a cheap shot at John Clifford. But it honestly isn't. The positioning that discourses do is experienced by each of us differently, and that's why I say I cannot speak for John. I *can* say, though, that I don't like what seems to me to happen to John, what his good-faith participation in this discourse makes him say. It's like watching a friend being bullied. If up to this point I've been trying, out of my considerable respect for him and his work, to empathize—to put myself in John's place, to see if maybe describing my life as he describes his in these terms might be acceptable, or at least not impossibly bad—now I can only sympathize and protest. "John," I want to shout, "don't let this discourse make you talk about yourself that way. You don't need to apologize in these terms! Better to be on the outside altogether—to be, for this discourse, one of the evil 'them' than such a marginal member of its 'us.'"

Naturally, the same kind of protest can be made—has been made, often—about the way the discourses of the Right position people: how people are constrained by seemingly commonsensical, everyday language that shapes perceptions of race or gender or class, for example. The charges leveled against such "hegemonic" discourses—most notably, perhaps, that they are largely incapable of critical self-consciousness—are serious ones. And, essentially by definition, it is the project of the Left to call such hegemony into question. The catch, though—and this is hardly an insight fresh with me—the catch is that it's very easy to simply replace one hegemony with another. That is, in order to create what it calls critical consciousness, the discourses of the Left may—for all I know, must—go beyond simply pointing out the interestedness of the discourses they oppose, to posit their own visionary privilege, their own insistent framing of what is "real." John Clifford tries to soft-pedal this tendency in the passage I've been working from—"a nonutopian attempt to raise the consciousness of a few," he calls his work—but I have also tried to show the price he pays for such restraint. In trying to suppress the discourse's hegemonic potential, he becomes its victim.

Ira Shor's writings, by contrast, suffer from no such restraint, and they seem to me, at least, to thereby harness far more of the discourse's considerable power—and at the same time to put into play much more of this hegemonic potential. When, for example, he defines liberatory education (to fill out the passage from "Educating the Educators" I've quoted a couple of times), he can afford to do so in far grander terms than John Clifford:

> Learning which is more than job training and more than socialization
> into subordinate lives seeks the critical study of society. Such education
> is a charmingly utopian challenge to inequality and to authoritarian
> methods, through a humorous, rigorous, and humanizing dialogue,
> with the April hope of lowering student resistance and teacher burnout,
> with the August desire of reknowing ourselves and history in that vast
> arena of culture war called education. (26)

Now that's an image that'll get you out of bed every morning! If you're going to be a soldier on this side in the culture war, this is the kind of soldier to be: humorous, rigorous, humanizing; chockful of sanctioned April hopes and August desires, anxious—as Shor says in another passage I've quoted from earlier—to get on with your "heroic efforts in the classroom" (*Critical Teaching* xiii). And it's made all the more attractive by contrast to what's left for those who might dissent: those of us grim dystopians who acquiesce to inequality and authoritarian methods, training our students for jobs, socializing them into subordinate lives.

Very likely, all discourses in any context have this hegemonic potential; anyway, I can't think of any I'm familiar with, from those of Catholicism to feminism to information theory, that don't. In this context, though—the context of this volume, the context of composition studies, the context of the way of life I've been sketching here—few discourses realize that potential as fully as this one. At its heart is the story of class struggle, of capitalism-in-inevitable-decline, generally attributed to Karl Marx and popularized by Friedrich Engels as "scientific socialism." Some 140 years have, to be sure, produced variations on this theme, variations obvious in just the contrast between the bits I've quoted from Shor and Clifford. But its basic premise seems to me essentially unaltered: that is, that the social, economic, and political inequities of our society cannot be meaningfully addressed by working through the system as it is — by way, for example, of conservative, or bourgeois, socialism. Only radical systemic change — revolution — can work: in particular, the elimination of capitalism as that system's foundation.

Such a discourse leaves little room for negotiation. If you're not part of the solution, as the slogan goes, you're part of the problem. These sharply differentiated poles, these insistent claims to visionary privilege, this framing of an agenda in such fundamental terms — always resonating for me, anyway, with that long-ago pledge to seek "the forcible overthrow of all existing social conditions" — make it a discourse that tends to be impossible to talk to; or one, at any rate, that never listens. It has an impressive terminological repertoire — notions like false consciousness, mystification, cooling out — with which to dismiss or denigrate all those other discourses of which my life is constituted. It seems unwilling to grant that any worthwhile hope or change, compassion or loyalty, any legitimate April hopes or August desires can spring from anywhere but itself. If we really are always already working within the discourses we encounter — if we can't, say, just change channels — then I find myself making the choice I urged on John Clifford, opting for a kind of discursive civil disobedience. Better to be an obdurate, full-fledged version of this discourse's "them" than to cut the deals — and make the denials — it would demand for me to be part of its "us."

There you have it. I can't — won't — use this language of the Left because it fails to describe my teaching; because it doesn't accord with the rest of my life; and, finally, because it presupposes a visionary privilege that I will not grant — emplots my life, if you will, in such a way that, forced to decide, I would choose to play the reprobate rather than the hero or, more likely, the apologetic tagalong. So why write this essay? Why join in an enterprise in which, at best, I'm likely to be viewed as ungracious?

Well, I have to return to what I said at the outset. People I respect and like describe their work in these terms. In spite of but also, however illogical it may sound, *because* of their use of this language, I think we have a good deal in common, a shared commitment to our students, our profession, our communities. In the spirit in which this volume was conceived, then, it is for them — to them — I have written here. What will they think? Maybe they'll say that I'm overreacting: that, to extend John Clifford's position a little, it is possible to share

goals and, for that matter, even tactics without sharing terminology—
that, in other words, I'm making far too much of what we used to be
able to call a matter of semantics. Maybe they'll argue that some or all
of my handling of the issues involved won't work: that, if nothing else,
there are languages and Lefts, but not—despite general usage—any
"language of the Left." Or maybe they'll even say that I've actually got
it right: that we really *are* on opposite sides of a serious political
divide; or, more optimistically, that while I'm right that our goals are
different, it may still be possible to share tactics, at least for a while.
Anyway, whatever they think, I look forward to finding out. Then we
can go on from there.

Works Cited

Clifford, John. "Review: Discerning Theory and Politics." *College English* 51 (1989): 517–32.

Elbow, Peter. "The Pedagogy of the Bamboozled." *Embracing Contraries.* New York: Oxford UP, 1986. 85–98.

Harris, Joseph, and Jay Rosen. "Teaching Writing as Cultural Criticism." *Drafts: Composition and Resistance.* Eds. Mark Hurlbert and Michael Blitz. Unpublished, 1989. 37–45.

Hurlbert, Mark, and Michael Blitz. "Prospectus: Composition and Resistance." Unpublished, 1988.

Shor, Ira. *Critical Teaching and Everyday Life.* Chicago: U of Chicago P, 1987.

———. "Educating the Educators: A Freirean Approach to the Crisis in Teacher Education." *Freire for the Classroom: A Sourcebook for Liberatory Teaching.* Ed. Ira Shor. Portsmouth, NH: Boynton/Cook, 1987, 7–32.

Berlin: You know what? I don't think I'm preparing them for the really good life. I mean they're going to have breakdowns. They don't understand that 50 percent of them are going to wind up divorced for instance, right? I mean, that's a statistic. The odds are that that's what's going to happen. In other words, we're not preparing them for this wonderful glorious future. I mean, it's not really that good a future anyhow, if they're going to be unhappy, right?

North: I don't think "right" is so simple an answer there, actually.

Berlin: What?

North: I don't think "right" is so simple an answer there.

Berlin: "Right?" What do you mean, "right?" What—

North: Is it right they're going to be unhappy. I don't think that's such a, I mean—

Berlin: I want them to know what's in store for them! I mean, they have narratives—

North: You're like an image broker. Here's a picture of poor people, here's a picture of unhappy rich people.

Berlin: No, I want to show them a picture of themselves in a few years and how unhappy they're going to be—

North: Well, you can't show that, you can't do that, you can only show—

Berlin: You can't?

North: You can give images. But you want a deeper response to a catalogue. You want something like a Sears catalogue—

Berlin: I want them to understand that what we've prepared for them, the good life for them is not really a good life.

North: Why?

Berlin: It's not all that good!

North: Why?!

Berlin: Why? Because they're not going—alright, their notion is that they're going to find peace and fulfillment and happiness, alright—

North: Are you sure?

Berlin: I'm sure. I'm absolutely sure—

North: I was an undergraduate at a state university, and I didn't have that image, so—

Stuckey: You didn't have to have it.

Berlin: No—

North: There you go. OK, why?

Stuckey: Because, you know, it's like made in America.

Mack: Mmmhmm!

Stuckey: You don't have to agree with it—

North: OK, so now I'm not—

Stuckey: And I don't really give a shit about personal fulfillment, especially for most kids who're going, you know, [to] either have it or not have it.

North: But—you're not—

Stuckey: But what you're talking about—well, I mean I don't want to be unhappy. I think there's a decent level of comfort to be achieved in life, and you can do it, and you can do it in all kinds of weird-ass ways if you ask me, but I'm not concerned about that in terms of what I think I'm doing. What I am concerned about is that this level of comfort rests on an extraordinary impoverishment of 33 percent of the people in the United States. And that most of the students that we're talking about in this room, it doesn't make a damn what we do with 'em. They're going to occupy those places in America that guarantee—

North: That's true.

Stuckey: —the impoverishment of the other 33 percent and I'm not willing—

Knoblauch: That's the problem.

Stuckey: —to participate in it, except of course, I do. Right? And I really don't like it but that's sort of what—it seems to me we're talking about in these articles.

14

This Desire for Change

C. Mark Hurlbert
Michael Blitz

As soon as one of the participants talked about an innovative practice, someone else pointed out that real resistance was unlikely within an institution and a society, which, as James Sledd put it, "serves the big bosses and their big money, and our institutional power structures are modeled after the corporations that they serve." A few participants expressed optimism. Quickly, others recalled that most, if not all, of the lofty aims typically advanced at conferences like 4C's were only improbably applicable to any of our day-to-day lives as employees of universities, colleges, and high schools. We were never far from acknowledging that we could, in the end, do little to change society if we could not arrive at a course of action for making real, lasting changes within our own departments and schools. And changing the politics of English departments did not, in spite of individually innovative classrooms and teachers, appear to be an inevitable outcome of educators doing good work. The participants resisted this concession, however, and perhaps we did so because we had all traveled many miles, at great expense, to meet with one another to do something *other* than merely complain about our jobs and to decide that teaching was a naively optimistic profession.

Hurlbert: I'm here in the perhaps fond hope that [as] we're talking, someplace else tonight there's another group of people talking, I mean—

Sledd: I don't think we even need to have a "fond hope."

Hurlbert: I mean there are people talking all over the country.

Sledd: Yeah, but I think the point is that, wasn't it Gramsci who talked about "optimism of the will and pessimism of the intellect," and since I taught Old English, I remember the Battle of Maldon, where the man said that "the weaker we get, the braver we have to be." So I don't see that hope is necessary. As a matter of fact, I think people who hope very much are crazy.

Blitz: I think a lot of people who have come to rely on a number of the names of people in this book, for one thing, will be shaken to find out that not everybody knows precisely what they're doing all the time. And one of the things that we [Mark and Michael] have been hearing from people who have asked us "Who's in the book?" is "Oh, what're *they* saying about resistance? What do *they* need to say about it?" And if you recall, those who were at the roundtable in Baltimore, I mean Berlin, for one thing, expressed great, loud, vocal doubts about virtually everything, and I think that's vital, to shake up some of the kinds of foundations that people have relied on in something called composition, which is hardly a composed discipline. And I think that's an important admission that the book is going to present. We're very doubtful, even about the purpose of the book itself. It *is* a book, after all. But I think that this book comes the closest, or *will* come the closest to a kind of admission of great possibilities for failure, and that's not a bad thing. It's making it necessary to get together to try to figure out, as Steve [North] suggests in his chapter, that it's time to see what can happen. This is the time. Elspeth, in your chapter, you suggest, following from June Jordan, that this is the time, this is exactly the time, it's the only time we have.

Stuckey: Yeah, that's the only thing, if you don't do it now—

North: You can't go back.

Blitz: And it's about time people would want to know that they can talk—

Hurlbert: That's the point of the question that Marion [Yee] gets and how she receives it. "Are you the teacher?" I mean, "Are *you* going to talk to us now?" And the kind of positioning that you [Yee] take in response to that.

What should we resist? How do we resist? Despite his misgivings about hoping for a better future in a troubled world, James Sledd spoke of the need to resist those who would control us and our students: "Often we *can't* resist. We have to be ready and watchful for the occasions when we can, and we have to accept the fact that nothing we can presently do will change anything much. Still, we have to try, because if everyone stopped trying, the worst would surely happen." We would be "crazy" to hope for change, but crazy if we didn't.

Mack: I think it's really important not to mystify change into something we can't do. I see that a lot of my students feel this inertia, that you can't change anything, I mean, we talked [at the Baltimore roundtable] about the contradiction. They're going to make these big salaries yet they can't solve problems. So as long as we allow change to be mystified, then people won't engage in it. And so I think it's really important that we have to do this local thing. I mean I'm about change all the time. Not just in my classroom and trying to figure it out, but in my relationships with other people, and I think it's important to bring all that in, and be role models and show all your doubt and how you're trying to

work this through. And I think it's really a lot more important what we do than what we say with our students—

Nearly All: Mmmhmm!

Mack: And, you know, to model this desire to change and be critical of what we're doing—hegemony has to do with coercion, that you don't have power—

Spellmeyer: That's right.

Mack: I mean look at all the composition teachers who are in the university. I mean we don't have any power. Well, you know we've got *lots* of power.

Hurlbert: Have you read Kathleen Weiler's book, *Women Teaching for Change*? She says that great thing about the value of being a utopian thinker or an idealist because she's got to have a reason to live tomorrow. And if we, and I guess I'm extrapolating from what she said, if we believers in the imagination want to *reclaim* the imagination. . .if we can't reclaim the imagination and believe that we can think of something better, of reimagining this whole damn mess we live in each day and then doing something about it, why the hell get up Monday morning? That's why, Elspeth, going back to what you said, that just, it knocked me out that you said that the two ends of this dichotomy really aren't in operation any longer. There's no point in throwing bombs in the United States, but we're not going to make big changes working in our little places—

Stuckey: Given the place that we already occupy. If we stay in the place that we occupy, then incremental change doesn't seem to me to do much more than sort of make perpetually good people doing good things and it doesn't change a damn thing.

Spellmeyer: I think being a self-reflective practitioner in a particular place is an opportunity for, for meaningful solidarities that translate into meaningful action.

Harris: And also the best you can hope for, I think. I mean, you can't transcend that sort of situation.

Mack: And so that's why all of this, this moment, is important to me, and that's why teaching composition, what I do, is also important. Writing and reading and dialogue have everything to do with being able to be self-critical of action. Which is every day. Which is local. Which can be collective.

What do we teach about writing when we write and talk about teaching writing? Nancy Mack asserted that critical actions can be collective. But Cecilia Rodríguez Milanés found, in relinquishing and then recovering control in her writing class, that individuals are always, also, acting in their own self-interests. As the Chicago roundtable ended, several people were concerned about how they were going to *appear* in the transcripts. As one participant put it, "There will be one part of me in this book over which I have considerable control. And another part over which I. . .in one sense lost all control once I uttered it." Control, in a project like this, is obviously a sensitive issue. But this concern is also an indication of a much larger problem we, Mark and Michael, noticed as we worked on *Composition and Resistance*: habits of speaking within the academy foreclose the possibilities for speaking in unfamiliar ways. To be fair, thinking out loud occasionally produces uncomfortable moments. We could not expect that all of the participants — or that we ourselves — would want all such remarks to be a matter of public record (which is particularly ironic since many see our discipline as devoted to the social dimension of composing). But the fact of the matter is that we came together to improvise and, as it turned out at the end, what we feared most were our most improvised remarks. Speaking from the imagination, rather than from the grounds of accepted conventions for professional conversations, requires a commitment to the dramatically unpredictable dimension of social events.

Sledd: If you sit out in the audience at these meetings [4C's] and listen to people talk, I've heard an astonishing amount of simple contempt for the high-flown talk about our "discipline." From people who I take to be, *whom* I take to be — sorry — teachers. And it seems to me that the discipline bit is just another way in which academics have *feathered their nests* —

Spellmeyer: Do you think —

Sledd: — and for real teachers, a lot of it is so much hokum.

Spellmeyer: Do you think that's *entirely* true? I think the situation is more complex than that. I think some of that resentment has to do with the off-putting character of a lot of theoretical language and the fact that theory often is used as a way of high-hatting people. But on the other hand, we owe it to ourselves and to our students to be self-critical. And I think that there is a certain kind of resistance to that. I was very distressed last year, for example, at Peter Elbow's talk ["The Problematics of Academic Discourse — Especially in Freshman Writing Courses" at CCCC, Seattle, 1989]. I don't know if you saw that. But basically it was pretty much theory-bashing. He was saying, "Well, who needs to ask these theoretical questions? They're just a kind of snobbery anyway. We know how to teach, we always have, it's almost instinctual." That's not the argument as you [Sledd] characterize it, but there, Peter had a standing ovation. There was a lot of resentment in that room, I think. Some of it was good-humored and some of it was *not* so good-humored, directed towards people who were raising the kind of questions that *we'll* be raising here, or have raised. And I think people will say of us, too, "Isn't this just another kind of academic exercise?" I think we have to be wary of, of, *not* being theoretical, too.

North: Even those of us who clearly disagree on, I guess what gets called "ideology," if you don't actually *not* talk, which hasn't happened yet, we *do* say, "Well, alright, what can we do in the Writing Center" or "How can we change this course, what can we do in a high school."

Mack: But I think part of this division [theory/practice, research/teaching] happens because we have this odd academic situation where people can exist within theory without teaching. And that's why there's such disregard for, you know, because what you're [North] talking about is sliding in and out of theory and practice all the time, in this movement to and fro, which I think is the way teachers operate, *good* teachers operate, *all* teachers operate. But there are some people who have this position of privilege who don't teach freshman comp, and maybe never did. And that just, that bothers me. And I think that bothers a lot of people, that there are people who are, you know, delivering papers and making statements who don't know what it's like and have no understanding of what the majority of people who teach composition do.

Reid: Isn't it also, doesn't it also make teaching composition respectable if there's disciplinary knowledge surrounding it—

North: Certainly is more money in it, yeah—

Reid: Well, I don't know about—

North: I don't know. If respectability's an issue, I guess—

Stuckey: Money *is* an issue, isn't it—

Reid: I mean, doesn't that make it like, it certainly isn't equal to teaching literature, right? [long pause]

Reid: I don't know. I mean, isn't, isn't part of the problem that I'm reading in the drafts [of the chapters] that teaching composition, especially teaching freshman composition, is not a respectable position. Right? So, does having disciplinary knowledge about something increase the respectability of the subject, is my question.

Spellmeyer: Well, I think it does, but it's at a terrible cost. [laughs]

Reid: Yeah!

Sledd: It seems to me icing on the cake. And it bugs me. Teaching composition is respectable whether people respect it or not! And if you think that in order to be respectable, you've got to go to conferences and write stuff in *College English* that I'm sure Jim Raymond doesn't understand, and I know I don't either, that seems to me to be utterly mistaken. There can be nothing more respectable than what we try to do. And if people don't respect it, well, you've got to put up with that, and maybe we can change their minds. But the notion that writing a big theoretical book makes the teaching of composition respectable strikes me as quite amusing.

Mack: I think it's buying into the belief system of the people who are already in power that "if you just try a little bit harder and do just a little more homework, they're going to give us more money and treat us better." There's no dean in the world who's going to hire composition teachers in a different way just because we have conferences and write papers and make books and torture graduate students with tests over this stuff.

Blitz: But there *is* a kind of insidious incentive plan intact that makes it possible, for instance, to have, for some individuals, the carrot of so-called "content" courses dangled before them if they do attend conferences and shape up in the discipline and absorb enough of the disciplinarity of composition that you go back to your home institution and you can certifiably claim, "I've been educated. I've attended this conference," or "I've attended a seminar or workshop held by somebody"—people we don't have to name to know who they are—and it becomes possible because it happens at my school, it's happened at Mark's school, where people have come back and said, "Yeah, I attended a workshop with so and so," and that enables them immediately to be permitted to propose another course that they might actually *like* to teach. And one of the functions of this shaping up as a "discipline" is that it deceives a lot of people, as you [Reid] suggest. I agree. I think a lot of people think that it *does* validate whole kinds of performances to have something that you can reliably call the "discipline of composition." Maybe that's something to specifically work against, or to confront, or question. Why is that part of the incentive plan? How did that happen? Why are people buying into it so readily?

North: I want to know if people sitting around a table talking about a book they're going to publish, I mean, are you going to make an institution out of questioning institutions—I mean you can, I don't know—I'm not sure you can have it both ways. Oh, you can have it both ways if you want to—

15

How We Apples Swim

James Sledd

What are we really doing at this conference?

Our assigned theme is "The Right to Literacy." The organizers have defined literacy broadly, in ads and announcements for the conference, as "the ability to use language in order to become an active participant in all forms of public discourse." So defined, literacy is impossible in the United States, and there can be no right to the impossible.

The proof of those wounding propositions is easy. Competent public discourse requires a large supply of general and special information; for without information, "the ability to use language" is only the ability to babble aimlessly. The assigned definition therefore requires that literates shall have not just a productive and receptive command of many linguistic registers in both speech and writing but also free access to needed information and free access to the media by which information may be exchanged. Those huge requirements are nowhere met. In the United States, the people who control the educational system and the media do not even want such free, informed, and general participation in public affairs.

To exemplify, consider first the familiar situation of a composition teacher—a big state university's primary worker for literacy. At the University of Texas at Austin, in many ways a representative institution, composition has been and still is mainly taught by underpaid but overworked graduate students and lecturers. They have only the smallest of voices in university governance, and administrators provide them only such information as the administrators choose. A few years ago, some fifty lecturers had to learn from the campus newspaper that

This essay was originally presented at the 1988 MLA Right to Literacy Conference.

their appointments would not be renewed for the following year. Too late for a hopeful job-hunt, they were simply set adrift. In the late spring of 1988, graduate students similarly learned from the campus newspaper what the administrators had known for weeks—namely, that the law would no longer allow the university to pay the students' insurance premiums. Without insurance, an already impecunious family could be ruined. Thus, by the definition established for this [1988 MLA "Right to Literacy"] conference—a definition which makes information essential to literacy—verbally gifted literacy workers at UT must be judged illiterate. They cannot participate actively even in discourse concerning their own work in a public university.

If literacy is confined to active participants in public discourse about university matters, then tenured and tenurable faculty at Texas are themselves by no means full literate. In getting and giving information relevant to their employment, they have difficulties comparable to those of the graduate students and part-timers, though less severe. Within the university, information flows mainly downward—when it flows at all. Administrators, and especially the higher administrators, have their newsletters and other brag-sheets. They have their wide network of administrative communication, national as well as local, and they can easily make themselves seen and heard in the newspapers and on radio and TV. They are the university's public voice, with an Office of Institutional Studies to provide them with whatever statistics may best suit their purposes. Faculty, on the other hand, speak publicly as private citizens only. They are well advised to limit voluntary communication with their academic superiors to channels established by the administrative hierarchy, and crucial information may simply be denied them. Rash souls who ask to see their own personnel files may not even be aware that administrators may first edit those files severely, and questions addressed to administrators in such bodies as the University Council may be evaded with doubletalk.

By the definition of literacy which has been assigned to us, illiteracy is indeed the prevailing condition of *all* citizens in the Land of the Free. In the recent past, congressional investigators were by no means able, even if they were willing, to learn in detail how a corrupt shadow-government made war on Nicaragua, in defiance of the citizens and their elected representatives. The former President and Vice-President of the United States went so far as to imply publicly that, by the MLA's definition, they too were illiterate. They did not know, they said, what was going on. The general tenor of their behavior makes that claim most plausible.

Perhaps a reminder is in order that the preceding examples of illiteracy *are* based on the MLA's own definition. Conferees must assume that the definition was carefully framed with an eye to its implications and that it is not a mere cover for hidden purposes. That obligatory assumption combines with the given examples to enable us now to say at least what we are probably *not* doing at this conference. Despite the assigned theme and the assigned definition of literacy, we are hardly participating, with the Modern Language Association, in "the building of a national upheaval" (Kozol). It is most unlikely that the moguls of the MLA have acquired a sudden interest in helping to work the deep social, economic, and educational changes which would be necessary to make active participation "in all forms of public discourse" open to everyone. For whatever mysterious reason, we are not abiding by the definition's undeniable implications.

The most plausible *affirmative* answer to the question what are we doing is then disheartening. Unless we do abide by the letter and spirit of the assigned definition of literacy, we are only serving ourselves, in disregard of logic. We are polishing apples and egos, padding our resumes, proving that "the ability to use language" without logical content is rightly characterized as the ability to babble. Some of us are babbling the catchwords of "cultural literacy," the contradictory, unworkable, and therefore much praised scheme which E. D. Hirsch has based on misunderstanding and misrepresentation of inadequate linguistic authorities. And as we serve ourselves, we may very well be impeding rational action by giving the false impression that rational action is already being taken. The wordy wars of inveterate conference-goers usually bring nothing else about.

If by some freak the conference *should* have some real effect, the emphasis on language in its definition of literacy is likely to be narrowly confining. If we teach the formal competencies of reading and writing to students who cannot hope for free access to information and the media, we may simply provide our bosses with another instrument of domination. Our bosses want a citizenry which is open to dictation. They want a "work force" which has been brainwashed into docility but which has the technical abilities from which the bosses profit. A true concern for literacy must therefore also be a concern for social revolution. But the MLA is not in the revolution business, no matter *how* it defines literacy.

I turn now from the conference and its organizers' puzzling choice of a definition of the literacy to which they affirm a right, and accordingly the pronoun *we* now shifts to a more restricted reference.

Only a fool would expect professors of English to lead a revolution; but some few small things we *can* do (if improbably we will). We should begin at home, in a sustained attempt to break the prevailing system of exploitation in our own departments — the exploitation of graduate students and part-timers, the general dislike for teaching composition, the general injustice to composition teachers. In the exploited, our effort would have the crucial support of an articulate group motivated by a genuine grievance.

Sue Ellen Holbrook's paper, "Women's Work: The Feminizing of Composition," at the 1988 meeting of the 4C's was a most articulate documentation of that grievance. Here is one paragraph from her abstract:

> Pedagogic in focus, its place in the curriculum conceived as "service" and elementary, extensively using paraprofessionals, allied with education departments and school teaching, and saturated by women practitioners, composition has become women's work. And so it will remain as long as those conditions remain. The transformation of composition from women's work to a sexually integrated and well-esteemed profession can come only as a part of the larger complex processes of raising the status of teaching itself and the other service occupations in a capitalist society, breaking down the sexual division of labor, achieving social and economic equity between women and men, and re-valorizing socially produced differences between the masculine and feminine genders.

The attempt, of course, to make the teaching of composition in the universities as respected as it is respectable would face the entrenched self-interest of many of our colleagues, the established literati who dominate the MLA. Even more frighteningly, it would face our country's whole damned and damning economic system—by which, to cite an outrageous instance, the University of Texas refuses ever to pay a tenured or tenurable composition staff yet can find millions and millions for the consortium known as the Microelectronics and Computer Technology Corporation and for the greedy band of corporations called Sematech, which the great Democrat Michael Dukakis tried to lure to Massachusetts.

Bruising experience teaches that such taxing and spending adversaries, like hard-core Reaganites, are inaccessible to rational conversation. Talkative conferences won't overwhelm corporate communities of knowledgeably grasping peers. Besides, the corporate executives control the accumulation, storage, and dissemination of knowledge and the media by which it is or isn't disseminated. Concerted action to escape that control, at least on one small academic front, would have to come before sane talking could even be heard. But if the MLA's professors are genuinely concerned for literacy, they ought to support such radical acts as loud resignations by directors of exploited composition staffs, equally loud refusals to fill the vacated directorships, unionization, repeated teach-ins in lower-division courses, well publicized demonstrations by teachers of composition and their students and friends, even strikes, walkouts, and the peaceful occupation of the offices of deans and presidents.

If such action did make at least a narrow gap in the prevailing limits on the thinkable and the speakable, then proponents of humanely employed literacy might make a successful appeal to the people. Parents alarmed by talk of a "literacy crisis" might be even more alarmed if teachers could tell them, openly and strongly, how little the higher-education establishment really cares for general literacy among an informed and active majority. The MLA might be prodded into *acting* on the implications of its definition of literacy.

Those proposals are very limited. They touch only that small proportion of the total population, mainly white, which makes its way to the big universities. Even so, to make them as the world now stands is to invite ridicule as a foolish dreamer. It may still be answered that ridicule is not reserved for the ridiculous. A society cannot reasonably demand that all students master its standard language unless the society gives them all a real chance to learn and use it and real rewards for using it well, and it is not contemptible to set one's own house in order before sermonizing one's neighbors. University professors of English do dominate the MLA.

Dominant professional attitudes, it has been said, not only guarantee but will continue to guarantee that teachers of English cannot contribute to significant social change but help instead and will keep helping to maintain the present unjust system of dominance and submission. The challenge to this conference is to refute that uncomfortable accusation, at least in some small way.

If we do not refute it, we should be required every day to con-template the old saying, "How we apples swim!" Tilley's *Dictionary of Proverbs* records Roger L'Estrange's exposition of it:

> Upon a fall of rain, the current carried away a huge heap of apples, together with a dunghill that lay in the watercourse. As they went thus, the horse-turds would be crying out still, "Alack a day! How we apples swim!"

Knoblauch: There's a serious trap in the assumption that we're dealing with institutional monoliths —

Mack: Mmmhmm.

Knoblauch: And we start with the belief that actually all of the power is situated in a handful of multinational corporations, and they are radically inaccessible to change. And what gets effaced is, for one thing, the reality of human agency in the world. That gets effaced. Suddenly we're merely passive before power-realities that we have no influence on, that we don't contest, that we're not — we can't be responsive to in any respect. And I think, I mean, any argument about social change is going to defeat itself to the extent that it, that it makes institutional monoliths of a social reality that is in fact changing all the time, every day, in intricate, tiny ways, and to the extent that it situates change at the level of some kind of grand revolutionary scheme rather than at the level of, you know, this situation and this one, and this one, and this one.

Berlin: So that's an argument for working in the classroom?

Knoblauch: That's an argument among other things for working in the classroom. And accepting the fact that the school is also a site for social change. It isn't just a preparatory ground for change that's going to happen someplace else or on a grander scale or whatever.

Berlin: Yeah, I'm very sympathetic to that point of view because anybody who's ever had a child in school understands the limits of his or her power, alright. You know, I feel like I might be able to change the ways that writing is taught in some parts of this country at the college level, but I'll never do anything for Happy Hollow Elementary School.

Reid: It sounds to me like the power to make changes comes from the power to speak, and if that's the case, then how does one get the power to speak and then how do we enable others to speak? But before we can talk about enabling others to speak, and make changes, I'd like to know what it is that gives people the power to speak. Is it awareness? Is it superior knowledge? Is it income? Is it what? And there are some things that we can't, that we can't enable students, I mean there are some things we can't do.

Berlin: Mmmhmm.

Reid: We can't change their income, we can't make them millionaires, probably.

Mack: So part of this is that we don't give students power, but we make them aware that they have that power. That's like the grammar issue. For a long time English teachers said, "If you just clean up your language, then people will listen to you," which is bullshit. [Students] should be listened to not some time in the future after they're out of the school-phony situation but now. I think that's part of the real problem that kind of puts together everything we've been saying. They have the power to create different lives for themselves, but they don't realize that. They're not authoring their lives. They're going through the paces, but they're not intentionally authoring their lives.

Golub: Ok, but let's take that idea. You're saying they have the power, they have this power but they don't realize it. That could be the same as not having the power. If we can make them aware of the power they do have, then all of a sudden — does that make sense?

Mack: Mmmhmm.

Singleton: About a third of my students come from East St. Louis. And when you talk about whether they know poverty situations, whether they have power or not...students come in and tell me, "I can't concentrate on my writing because my neighbor was shot and her child was shot through the head last night." Their future may not be wonderful, but their present stinks, you know, right now.

Berlin: Yeah, right.

Singleton: And so part of their life is having some dreams, some hope that maybe, if they can get out of basic writing and maybe get into 101, and maybe survive 101's exit final, maybe they can get into some "real" courses that they've been paying for, for maybe two years. Part of *us* are paying for it too. A lot of them are on Pell grants and things. Then maybe they can get that accounting degree and maybe get a better job than working at Hardee's. So it's a real, a real tough situation to convince them that they have power, because they haven't had power in schools. They haven't had any power, and they're living next to a crack house in East St. Louis. It's a real different situation than what I hear you all talking about.

Mack: But we have to be really careful that we aren't selling that—"a college education gives you power."

Singleton: No.

Mack: And Michael, you and I have this in common, teaching inmates. And one of the things that I got wised up to right away was trying to pass off a college education as a panacea, that this would make their lives better. It doesn't necessarily happen that way. I guess I could say for most of my students in prison that it wasn't going to get them a better job at the end.

Berlin: Right.

Singleton: I'm trying to decide that maybe they need to just deal with where they are right now, and maybe the biggest thing that they need to write about is to write because they're mad that the financial aid screwed up their loan—

Mack: Great.

Singleton: —and misread their social security number, so they had to borrow money from aunt so-and-so, so that they could come back to school the next quarter, and so they wrote an essay to me about it, and I said, "Why don't you send this to the financial aid people or to the president? They're worried about retention, they're especially worried about retention of black students at this school because the enrollment is dropping so radically, and why don't you do something about it?" Other students were really honked off that their TA's in math classes were non-native speakers, and [these students] couldn't understand math, and they certainly couldn't understand it from a non-native speaker [whose English] they couldn't understand at all. And so I said, "Write about this." And they wrote about it, and I said, "Ok, do you want to do more with it?" And they said, "Oh, no. That wouldn't help. It wouldn't get anything done." And I said, "Well, I know the person on the committee that's supposed to review these. They have to fill out a form on me, that I can speak English well enough to teach this class. So somebody is making somebody care about it."

It was interesting 'cause [one student] wrote the paper and decided to turn it in to this [committee] person. First she wanted to make posters and put them up because that would have more effect, she thought, to get other students riled up than to turn it in to some university official. And so they did it. But until I did all this nudging, she didn't feel that she had *any* power. They feel very powerless. What good would it do? So they'd rather just turn in these little essays just to me, and —

Berlin & Mack: Mmmhmm!

Singleton: — and "tell me what you want me to do, I want to get on, I want to get this degree."

Mack: What a beautiful example. That just says everything we've been talking about. I think that's a beautiful example about how it's not for some future situation, it's for right now.

Singleton: Because I can't promise that they're going to get their grant next quarter. All's I can do is what we're doing right here.

Mack: That's scary stuff —

Rodríguez Milanés: Or that they'll come back alive —

Singleton: Right.

Reid: And it doesn't take many of those successes to make them feel like they can make a change, but it takes hundreds of A's for some kids to feel like they're good writers. But, you know, my kids are writing letters to get the bus stop changed, and some kid the other day said, "Guess what! They're going to stop at my stop!" I mean, so I really don't care that he has to walk half a mile less, but he was so happy that he had done this thing, and it doesn't take much of that, to make them feel —

Harris: I think that's a great story, but there are some things about it that bother me, which is precisely that somehow the work in the classroom is validated by writing or discourses taken outside the classroom. Even your [Singleton's] phrase, to the effect of, you know, instead of writing these "little essays to me," I mean there's a way in which — I don't like that phrasing — but it seems to me that writing little essays to me, the teacher, can have a powerful, worthwhile, and critical, liberatory effect. Part of the work students can be doing can be serious academic work. They can be learning critique and that *how* you do that and *where* that's applied is what's in classrooms, largely. When my students learn how to do it well, as they occasionally do, I'm really pleased, and my next move is not to say, "Gee! if only this had a real-world application" — I think there's a trap there.

Singleton: But I find that my students can't do the other...for an academic purpose with any sense of feeling about it. They just don't care because it doesn't mean anything to them. Whereas some of these other things are real issues. It's like they need the training ground on something that they care about. Otherwise they're just doing this little thing to please me. But I don't negate what you're saying because sometimes just having..., writing a journal that I read and dialogue with them is validation of their voice, and they've never had anybody just read without putting the grade on something. And so not everything has to be sent to the president of the university for it to have any effect. I guess I was just saying that for those students, it's good just to be heard sometimes. That's what some of my students need—just to be heard. But it's good for them to feel that they can write about something that really honks them off and that they need to do something about it. Even though they didn't feel they had the power to do, and I don't *make* them take the letter to the president. I don't make them do those things. I try to nudge them into seizing some of that power that could be theirs if they chose to do it.

Harris: I agree very strongly with what you're saying. I guess one thing I'm reacting against or responding to, is a sort of uneasiness with simply doing what it is that I see myself largely spending my time doing, and I'm quite happy with doing, and that's sort of my point. Which is, to try to involve college freshmen seriously with academic work. Along these lines, I think, and viewed in the context of the larger culture, that much academic work can be in serious ways resistant, critical, to offer options that otherwise aren't there. There is a view of the university, in other words, that—it's a largely fictional one—I'm willing to represent and stand for. And it seems to me that that is hard work, and it seems to me to be good work, and it seems to me that we're continuing trying to say, "Well, we have to push beyond that, we have to do that and work for social change, too" or whatever. I, I don't feel that way—

Berlin: Yours is political discourse, Joe come on. I mean, you know, Donna's talking about political discourse—I mean you had them analyze the media which constantly has designs on them.

16

Transforming Composition
A Question of Privilege
Nancy Mack
James Thomas Zebroski

Does the Remedial Writer Have a Place in Academe?

Nancy: I feel certain that unless there are radical changes in the social structure, students will continue to exist who do not write well, particularly students who do not write and speak the prestige dialect. Whether the university decides to deal with these students or not is a political decision of great importance. Enrollment numbers for remedial students are dramatically affected by the university's position on issues such as student loans, tuition fees, textbook prices, entrance requirements, placement testing procedures, the means of funding remedial courses, staffing policies, the number of sections offered, and so on. Compositionists tend to avoid these difficult political issues and prefer instead to concern themselves with issues that will improve instruction in the individual classroom. Yet, composition teachers often carry out policies that help to manage the official numbers of remedial students. For instance, as anyone who has graded placement tests knows, there are pressures to slide the scores one way or another in order to make the enrollment numbers in various level courses come out right — whatever "right" is that particular year.

Jim: I'd like to draw attention to the historical dimension of this problem. We must remember that the university hasn't always embraced the marginal student. The university was first presented with a large student population who needed remedial writing courses during the heady, open admissions days of the 1970s. We soon learned to use the euphemism "basic writers" to label these students. It was more pleasant

154

to focus on writing performance as the main difference between the remedial students and the traditional students than it was to acknowledge that this new group of students came from racial and social-class groups who before this time did not have easy access to the university. The university seems content to have the income from these students, yet at the same time the university finds these students to be an embarrassment to its elite image of itself.

Nancy: The real question here seems to be whether the university has any commitment to teach these students. It is one thing to put in place social programs that allow these students entry into the university, but it is quite another thing to provide quality programs that will enable these students to graduate. A real commitment to educating these students would mean staffing remedial programs with well-trained, full-time, tenured professors. A university is a complex social institution with many policies and procedures that must be altered in order to make the university more democratic. Providing loans for low-income students and scholarships for black athletes are false promises if the university has no intention of making sweeping changes in everything from its curriculum to its staffing policies.

Jim: When we turn our backs on these students, we never do so because they come from marginal racial or social-class groups. We always do so because of the numbers. Numbers provide us with the handy smoke screen of neutrality. We tell the students that it's nothing personal, but they just don't have the right test scores or grade points to be admitted or retained in the country club community of academe.

Nancy: In other words, discussing their perceived cognitive deficiency is considered acceptable whereas discussing their perceived social deficiency is not.

Jim: I must point out that marginalization is itself a social construct no matter whether we use writing samples, test scores, or blood pressure readings to determine the students' relative status to the privileged group. Accordingly, the remedial students' struggle to be accepted by the university is not just an academic struggle; it is a social struggle as well.

Nancy: I am continually amazed that the process of marginalization works so smoothly. I watch working-class students quietly leave the university without uttering a peep in rage at the institution. They blame themselves rather than the university for their failings. They rarely make a scene in someone's office. They never rail against the lunacy of sitting in a class of 400 students, having their tests graded by machines. Instead, they go home, cursing their own stupidity or laziness. I have a hard time considering my students lazy when the majority of them work one or more jobs and many of them are parents of small children. I like your use of the word *struggle*. My students struggle in ways that people from the upper class could never understand.

Jim: Ironically, even when working-class students are successful, they do not feel that their success is legitimate. Sennett and Cobb make this point in *Hidden Injuries of Class*. Working-class students often discredit their role in their own success by crediting their good fortune to luck or to the mercy of the teacher. Thus, working-class students end up praising their teachers for their good grades while faulting themselves for their bad grades. In both situations, the students give the power of legitimization over to the institution.

Nancy: Even more so than instructors in other disciplines, composition teachers certify which students are acceptable to the academy. Our job is to sort out those students who do not meet the university's standards from those who do. Somewhere along the line, equality and meritocracy get all mixed up.

In America we like to believe in a limited form of equality — equality at the starting line but not at the finish line. We believe that all people have an equal chance at making something out of themselves. We justify the inequality at the end as just a measure of the fact that some people work harder than others. The people who are chosen to be successful supposedly deserve more because they merit it. Our competitive culture is based on a belief in the fundamental inequality among people; we believe that some people should be privileged over others.

Can Working-Class Students Make Language Speak for Them?

Jim: So it would seem to follow that composition teachers should teach working-class students the prestige dialect in order that they can earn the privilege to be heard. However, the issue is so much more complicated than just the decision whether or not to teach Standard English to those who are judged as nonstandard.

Nancy: Of course, we should teach the dialect of the privileged group to working-class students, but we should stop promising that this single feat will make them acceptable to those in power. To do so grossly oversimplifies the politics of language. Language is one arena where thousands of social-class struggles can be witnessed. As Mikhail Bakhtin tells us, words do not get their meanings from dictionaries. Each group speaks its intentions into words; accordingly, the meanings of words live through a semantic tug of war as one group pulls the word nearer to its meaning and vice versa. The history of this perpetual tug of war is seldom discussed in composition classes. We deal very little with the politics of language beyond making vapid promises of wholesale upward mobility.

Jim: Then wouldn't it follow that if we teach working-class students the dialect of the wealthy, we would in part be teaching them the ideology of the upper class?

Nancy: Yes, this is indeed a danger. Ideology permeates the words, structure, and content in writing. Therefore, certain ideas are easier to express in Standard English than others. For instance, the five-paragraph theme format lends itself to discussing a pseudoreality which is far removed from the pain of the working-class students' everyday lives. In the process of learning to write, many working-class students are alienated from having anything to say—from speaking for themselves. Language learning becomes harmful when the student loses his or her integrity to say something of significance in the process.

Jim: However, this need not be the case. The way we teach writing does not have to alienate the working-class student from his or her lived experiences. It is our conception of language that makes all the difference. If we portray language as a rigid, right-or-wrong rule system, the working-class student has no choice but to assume a passive position to the elite language. In opposition to this, Bakhtin's conception of language allows the student to assume an active position to language. Bakhtin portrays language as dynamic and ever-changing, a social dialectic that responds to the material reality of interacting groups.

Nancy: Then the goals that the remedial composition teachers dangle in front of their working-class students would have to change. The carrot would no longer be the illusion of upward mobility but instead would be the desire to make language speak for the working-class students' needs and interests.

Jim: Working-class students need to actively write themselves into the language. They do not realize that they are already part of the Bakhtinian dialogue. Part of the process of being heard by society, taking a place in the dialogue, is transforming the language. Working-class students must continually push and pull at language in order to make the language speak for them and their reality, since by its very nature the elite language speaks best for the more wealthy, traditional college student.

Nancy: Yes, remedial students usually end up spending all their energy trying to pass for the elite social group rather than attempting to speak out for themselves and their social group. Paulo Freire wanted the peasants to become their own leaders. This notion is remniscent of Antonio Gramsci's concept of the organic intellectual. Gramsci had the belief that the working class needed to grow its own intellectuals rather than continually borrowing them from the liberals in the upper class. Organic intellectuals have the benefit of two types of education. They are educated in the daily reality of the lived experience of their social class, and they are educated in the school-represented culture of the prestige group. After receiving both forms of education, the organic intellectual can best lead his or her social group.

Jim: This is an important point because this is where a lot of people misunderstand critical consciousness. Critical consciousness is not simply the act of becoming indoctrinated with the ideology of the well-meaning, liberal, upper-class teachers. Critical consciousness is when a person speaks out for the interests of a social group of which he or she is a member. A student cannot learn someone else's critical consciousness.

Nancy: I do not want my students to fit into the existing society; I want them to transform society so that society is more responsive to their human needs. Although I encourage my students to make society more democratic, I must admit that the university is probably one of the least democratic social institutions. As a work environment there is probably more race, class, and gender discrimination at the university than there is at General Motors.

Jim: This makes the university one of the prime candidates for transformation by the working-class students. If we're going to let them into the university, then we also have to let in their ideas, and ultimately we have to let them into the language as well.

Nancy: We should be careful not to imply that working-class students are not already changing language all on their own without the aid of the liberatory composition teacher. It is a little pompous to assume that we are the ones to begin this process. All marginalized groups create their own words and meanings, which then may be borrowed by the status quo. For instance, from my experience teaching prison inmates, I learned that many popular slang phrases such as "shakedown," "homeboy," and "funky" originated in the prison. By not acknowledging the fact that the students from marginal groups already have the ability to change language, the composition teacher further renders these groups powerless. Sometimes I wonder if composition teachers so enjoy being the agents of empowerment that they emphasize the remedial students' powerlessness so that they will want to become empowered.

Jim: Likewise, it would be very ridiculous to assume that we are the only purveyors of critical consciousness to the working class. Working-class students already have many insights about the ways that they are being ripped off by the upper class.

Nancy: Once again, the academy gives itself the position of privilege. We've got all the critical consciousness. How far away are we from offering courses in remedial critical consciousness? University professors are great know-it-alls. We have to leave room for the students to know something — to know more than we do. Students must feel that they have something to say. This issue is what makes language learning meaningful and what gives the student the need to transform the language and the university.

Have Working-Class Students Changed the Field of Composition?

Jim: I want to move the discussion on into the area of the status of composition as a field or discipline that is related to the history and fate of the remedial composition student that we have been attending to. To an important extent composition as a legitimate area of specialization and scholarship in the American university arose because of open admissions and the subsequent influx of working-class students into the elitist university. That, matched with the glut in the job market for literature Ph.D.'s during the 1970s, made composition as a field possible.

Nancy: This is not to say that people did not study writing before this time. Many people worked hard to establish the study of writing as important, intellectual work during the 1950s and the 1960s. But the institutional legitimacy of composition, if it came at all, came with the turmoil of the student protests of the sixties and the demands for equality and democracy in the educational system. Composition gained special attention when these newcomers arrived at the university. At a time when remedial writing programs at these elite universities are being or have already been quietly dismantled, we need to consider the origins of these programs and question whether conditions warrant their termination.

Jim: It amazes me that we now have volumes of excellent scholarship in composition tracing the connections between composition/ rhetoric and the academy a hundred or two hundred years ago, but we still have very few studies examining the role that composition played in the late sixties and early seventies in introducing the open-admissions students to the university. Composition was (and is) the only course required of all students. It is the first (and for various reasons, often the only) course in which the world of the student meets the world of the academy. We need to keep in mind that one of the reasons composition as a field may be different is that it arises on the borders between worlds. In an age of excellence, too often a code word for elitism, the significance of this clash of social groups seems to be overlooked.

Nancy: Bakhtin's analysis of language revels in this heteroglossia of language. Bakhtin explains how this dialogue between various social strata creates a living language. He discusses how genres and whole disciplines arise on the borders and in the mixedness, in the institutional and discursive "between spaces." Bakhtin points out that it is the so-called lower social strata who enliven and enrich the elitist and fossilized institutions by dialogizing them—by even carnivalizing them.

Jim: Yet, the first-year composition course still puts these working-class students under a great deal of pressure to pass—to talk and write like we do—to become, so the myth goes, one of us. The implication is this: We will allow you into our club if you just give up your identity and talk and write like us. The irony of this is that, to a greater extent than anyone I know seems willing to acknowledge, working-class students have made and continue to make the field of composition. Thus, composition's dramatic changes in the last two decades have much to do with a new dialogue between the university and the working class. And yet there still remains this urge to convert them, to make them acceptable to the group who has the most to learn from the working-class student.

Nancy: But you have to admit that this relationship has been somewhat dialogic. The working-class student could only have had such a large impact upon the field of composition if the compositionists were willing to listen, in fact were willing to transform what they knew in order to think about the very activity of composing in different ways. What other discipline in the university changed itself for working-class students as much as composition did? Part of all the talk about product versus process was about the discipline rethinking itself, engaging in dialogue and transforming itself and to a lesser extent transforming the university. And all of this occurred because composition teachers were committed to helping the working-class student to succeed in the university.

Jim: Maybe. But that raises the whole issue of why we are teaching composition. Is it to help working-class students transcend their world or to transform it? Do we simply want them to move on up into the academic world and then into the business world?

Nancy: That's true; being successful usually means little more than fitting into the existing system, as you mentioned before. This is why composition must avoid accepting the role of a mere service course, sort of the washerwoman of the university—scrub up these untidy students so that the other disciplines can do their work with the least degree of change.

Jim: Your metaphor of a washerwoman is very appropriate since it is mainly women who labor as teachers in these first-year composition courses.

Nancy: I was more concerned with representing the discipline of composition as subserviant to the other disciplines. To use another metaphor, composition initiates the new students into the fraternity of academe — teaching them the secret semicolon handshake and the like.

Jim: Perhaps more problematic than the relative status of composition to the other disciplines is the underlying notion that the academic language is monologic. Writing across the curriculum could become nothing more than a unilateral movement to make all science majors speak like science majors should. A better idea might be to let the science majors in on the centrifugal forces in their discipline. For instance, how do the languages of James Gleick, Rachel Carson, Carl Sagan, and Albert Einstein add to the diversity of scientific language? We make a discipline inert by neutralizing the drama of the ongoing conflicts of opposing groups. Every discipline needs the vitality of these conflicts to keep it from becoming a dead corpse.

Nancy: This is why transformative teaching is more rigorous than traditional teaching. The many languages of academe become the focus of language study. The teacher and the students read and write and study about these issues. Moreover, there are several important reasons for including the diverse languages of the students in the fray. First of all, their slang, dialects, second and third languages are all worthy of respect in themselves. Of all people, we as language experts should celebrate this fact. Second, student languages should be valued as a necessary part of the dialogue. There cannot be a dialogue when, from the very beginning, students are silenced with the criticism that their languages are inferior. Finally, the languages from outside the academy should be solicited because those languages, given half a chance, have the potential to interrogate reigning languages and reigning ideas; they are sources of resistance. Returning to the topic of disciplinarity, these languages have the potential to transform the discipline we are constructing.

Jim: So, the cutting edge of composition as a discipline lives in the first-year composition course where these languages are still the most lively?

Nancy: That is certainly one of this field's most important edges. Some people think of teaching freshman composition as drudgery. I like it because these students are the least indoctrinated into the university. First-year students are borderline people who are in and between two worlds. That, according to Bakhtin, is precisely the space where language development is the strongest and most vital, or at least potentially. Being on the borders gives a very different view of things than being at the center.

Jim: The academy desperately needs that vision, but not in order to make bigger and better clones of itself but in order to transform its vision of itself. So, composition as a discipline could benefit from accepting social class as central to its own creation and development.

Nancy: This is very much in the spirit of Bakhtin. Dialogue for him is not some parlor game. It is not: Let's talk until I win. Rather, it is: Let's talk until you change not only what I say and think, but who I am.

Jim: Composition should not try to be like other, well-established disciplines or fields of study. If we try to measure ourselves by the standards of elite, "pure," "modernist," disciplines, we will not only always fall short by their measure but we will cut ourselves off from our very sources of life. Also, I do not think that it is very useful to aggrandize composition as a metadiscipline that transcends and binds together the worlds of academe. Nor is it useful to view composition as a subdiscipline that is a foundationalist discipline, something everyone needs, like a minimum daily allowance of vitamins. Instead, I like to think of composition as the interstices between worlds, the place where worlds meet and often, given the kind of society we live in, collide. Composition is borderline (in many ways). However, we should keep our borders as porous and permeable as possible.

Can Composition Be Transformed?

Nancy: This borderline or mixed quality is an important feature of the discipline of composition. This quality also reminds me of the experience that we had writing this article together.

Jim: We first became interested in writing a dialogue because of our past history of years of pursuing the same topics in composition theory and in our classrooms. In a way, this article came from hundreds of hours of dialogue, first starting in graduate school, that has kept our scholarship alive.

Nancy: Keeping theoretical interests alive after graduate school is really difficult. No matter what university a person is located at, it is hard to find the time and the people to talk with who are interested in the same things. It is also very important to do a lot of reading and rereading of key works together.

Jim: Yes. In fact reading Bakhtin several times has been important in our consideration of the social nature of language.

Nancy: It is interesting how his notion of the dialogic quality of words impacted the writing of this article. This article was not written with you writing your words or me writing my words. It was not edited down from a transcript of a tape of a single conversation. Instead, we each wrote sections of this piece with one person writing the interchange between both speakers.

Jim: We weren't writing a play with each character having a clear persona in comparison to another character. We were more concerned with the dialogic quality of the words themselves. Although we chose a genre that credits certain lines to one individual at a time, any quotes taken from this dialogue should be credited to both of us. We have considered these ideas many times for a long period of time. The ownership of these words gets blurred in the dialogue.

Nancy: Particularly key words like *transformation*, *privileged*, and *dialogue*. These words no longer have a discrete territoriality. They have become so essential to our dialogue that they belong to both of us and to others who are not named here. Sometimes when we used a word I could really hear someone else's voice in that word. As Bakhtin says, the word was charged with an alien word.

Jim: Of course, this is where the arguments came in. We shouldn't portray this dialogue as all sweetness and light. When we quarreled it wasn't about who said what but whether a word could or could not be used to describe something.

Nancy: For example, we had real problems with the word *ownership*. I kept pushing for using this word while you resisted.

Jim: This is in part because the word brings to mind concepts of property and capitalism. The word can also be turned back upon the field of composition when we ponder who is entitled to have ownership over its development.

Nancy: And we could question who has ownership over the individual article, essay, or theme. In our case, this article was not written just for fun or, worse, because it was an assignment. We wrote it to speak for issues that are important to a small group of scholars.

Jim: Speaking for a collective complicates things. Not everyone in the group would be willing to phrase things as we have.

Nancy: Which brings us back to why *ownerhip* is such a sticky word. I want to push the word *ownership* beyond its individualistic meaning to embrace a collective application. When an individual makes a commitment to write a statement for a group, ownership goes through an interesting dialectic. The person feels ownership individually and becomes willing to argue with others about the use of key ideas and words. At the same time, the person experiences ownership collectively by writing this for others, a social group who may or may not be present.

Jim: This collectivist writing could be done alone or with someone else, but it still must represent the integrity of a larger group. A commitment to transformation is what draws people together and makes it necessary to write something in the first place. In this context, individual words are worth fighting over for social reasons.

Nancy: This sounds a lot different from the current notion of collaborative writing. In many institutions including the university, collaborative writing is made into an antisocial experience where the real messiness and disputatious quality of the dialogue is socialized into a neutral message. The conflict and disharmony not only makes things interesting, it gives the writing a reason for being.

Jim: It is also much different from most assignment writing, which trivializes the motives for authorship. It's difficult to feel like an author in a traditional composition course because nothing is really being created, nothing is being transformed, no one has any integrity.

Nancy: The older generation always seems to want the same old thing replicated in their honor rather than letting the younger generation create something new. In composition courses, we are too concerned about getting students to replicate the old conventions, the accepted formats, and the sanctioned topics. When we overdo this desire to replicate ourselves in our students, we undermine their authority to speak up and make changes. The study of composition should give the student the privilege the author both the word and the world.

Jim: Composition should see itself as rooted in the future, not simply saddled with the task of passing on an elitist tradition from the past. I want my students to create a language and a world view and a world that I cannot begin to conceive of. And I want the students, who are interested in doing so, to go on to study in composition and then change this field and its place in the university.

Works Cited

Bakhtin, M.M. *The Dialogic Imagination*. Ed. Michael Holquist. Trans. Caryl Emerson and Michael Holquist. University of Texas Press, Slavic Series, No. 1. Austin: U of Texas P, 1981

Sennett, Richard, and Jonathan Cobb. *Hidden Injuries of Class*. New York: Random House, 1973.

Vološinov, V.N. *Marxism and the Philosophy of Language*. Trans. Ladislav Matejka and I.R. Titunik. Cambridge, MA: Harvard UP, 1986.

Harris: We can start thinking about ways of getting them [students] to stop dealing with themselves as, say, consumers of knowledge, and [to begin seeing themselves], in some ways, as co-creators of knowledge, which is where writing, it seems to me, becomes particularly handy. And again, what's frustrating me about, you know, I don't know whether it's a demand for technique or whatever, but I mean, the question of how to get people to do that seems to me to be a very complicated and interesting one, and I think people in their essays began to talk abut that short of stuff, but I would love to continue that kind of talk, in a sense get past what strikes me, despite all of our good intentions, is a kind of vast prolegomena to that talk.

Singleton: So we can erase the tape? And start over?

Blitz: I would suggest that, Joe's point...that we've been rehearsing a pro-legomena is not entirely, not all *all* a bad thing.

Harris: Mmmhmm.

Blitz: I mean, I sensed a critical tone in what you said, Joe, but I think finding a place to begin is the best possible thing I can see working with this group of people, or any group of people, to do. I'm interested in the fact that we've now had four or five hours together to figure out where to begin, and I have a feeling that we might actually begin to know where to *begin*, which might be to find...I think story telling might actually be one of the ways—

Spellmeyer: Yes—

Blitz: Donna Haraway has a wonderful new book on Primatology that just came out, a professor at Santa Cruz in anthropology. She studies the history of studying primates, and one of the points she makes is that we've studied them so aggressively and so furiously just to figure out whether we resemble ourselves? [laughter] And if we don't, what do we look like? We don't look like *them* anymore. And the prostheses of the future—television, telephones, artificial limbs—they don't resemble *us*, and we don't resemble them. We don't resemble ourselves anymore, and so she proposes that primatology's most important and fascinating function is that it has allowed us to tell elaborate stories about ourselves and then read them again—

Berlin: Right.

Blitz: And then every time you read them, something—she calls it magic—she says something magic happens. And she locates magic between logic and desire, and I think we're, we're trying to, I really felt that toward the end of this, I want very badly for something magical to happen now, because I have strong desires to not have people die outside the building I teach in, and I also have to think very logically, too, about the limitations of doing much about that unless I start someplace. And I think this is, I'm happy this is where, one place I'm starting, after all these years. Isn't that a reason to do this?

Hurlbert: I think we've talked about, we've talked about in our essays and in our roundtables, how to live with ourselves and how to create classrooms in which our students can better choose the selves they want to be. I mean, this is essential work.

Mack: I think a lot of people feel that one of the great harms of working with students and talking about critical consciousness is that you leave them with no hope and great depression. And I think I went through phases of that myself, and still do periodically. But I think that I became increasingly aware, thinking about being here, and then being at the conference, that I was doing this a lot for just me. I mean, this is as good as it gets for me. To be able to be in a room with people who are thinking along the same lines as I am when, on the job, most of the time, I don't have that kind of contact. This is real important for me, and it's real important for me to challenge what I think. But I don't know about being able to say that we're going to make radical changes as soon as this hits the—fan!

17

Class Actions

Michael Blitz
C. Mark Hurlbert

At the Baltimore roundtable, Louann Reid said, "It sounds to me like the power to make changes comes from the power to speak, and if that's the case, then how does one get the power to speak and then how do we enable others to speak? But before we can talk about enabling others to speak, and make changes, I'd like to know what it is that gives people the power to speak. Is it awareness? Is it superior knowledge? Is it income? There are some things that we can't, that we can't enable students, I mean there are some things we can't do."

In what ways do we learn about the power to speak? The two of us realized, when we were reading over early drafts of the chapters, that this is precisely what the participants seem to be working on in their own teaching. Cy Knoblauch creates a classroom context for students to discuss, to perhaps come to terms with, their own privilege and power. Cecilia Rodríguez Milanés openly examines with her students the problematics of speech and power within a classroom community. And Donna Singleton questions how academic policies and practices support the efforts of those who try, however unconsciously, to prevent her from speaking with the authority she knows she has. Our classrooms are places to learn about the power to speak by speaking and writing, by watching what happens when we do, and by seeing what we and our students can do as a result of our writing(s). Or they could be. In *The Politics and Poetics of Transgression*, Peter Stallybrass and Allon White argue that taking "Control of the major sites of discourse is fundamental to political change" (202). If the teaching of writing and literature is to be about real political and social change, it will have to include helping students to see how writing creates, just as it results from, contexts for acting. Teachers can call attention to the experiences of other people who are struggling. Teachers can encourage students to *make* something of their research. Writing teachers, in both composition and literature classrooms, have the power to open writing up by helping students to see how actions become possible as a result of writing.

One of us asked students to write hypothetical narratives about homeless people. We then went to talk with Donald, "Bat," and Rowanda, who had been living outside our classroom building, on the subway grating, for the past several months. We also asked two others, Mike and a woman who asked us to call her "Number 1," to join us. Mike and "Number 1" had been living in an elaborate box-tent across the street in a corner of an unfinished construction site. Twelve students, one teacher, and five homeless people talked about a kind of struggle that many of us might hear *about* but which few people in higher education have an opportunity to listen *to*. Students distributed copies of their narratives and listened to reactions and comments. Later, students wrote up a comparative report, including the original narratives along with quotes from Donald, "Number 1," Rowanda, Mike, and "Bat." These reports have been sent to the Mayor's office and to the State Department of Human Resources. And, following one student's lead, we sent copies to several major developers, including Donald Trump. In addition, the students proposed that the school newspaper include a regular feature of some kind dealing with homeless people, perhaps written by a homeless person.

One of our classes collectively wrote a book on violence at our campus, which included interviews with victims of campus violence, analysis of and suggestions for crime prevention, reports on places for victims to get counseling, and calls for administrative action. The students sent this book to the president of the university. Another class wrote a book on alcohol use and abuse on campus, which members of a campus outreach program requested in order to, among other things, create a more convincing annual budget request to the State. In all of these activities, students find ways to make what they write and learn accessible to others in a powerful way. In actions such as these, students see how writing can itself be an act to change the way that people think about living in the world—which may be one of the only ways we have to change the world.

If we are really committed to political, social, and economic change, we must also stand as better examples of collective work in our teaching. We can start by breaking out of the one teacher—one class mode of education. Perhaps we can enact a new form of team teaching, where teachers move around from class to class or where classes join other classes in projects as advisors, collaborators, and co-evaluators. We can plan ways to have groups of teachers and theorists in classes. If the formats for dialogue and presentation at the major conferences represent

educators' collective preferences, why not introduce more of a conference format into our daily work? Why not include students in such a
format? Why don't more teachers ask students what it is they think
they need to be taught and what they think about the things they have
already been taught? In graduate education, we need to argue for the
legitimacy of collaborative writing. We need to claim a place, for
instance, for collaborative dissertations in our universities and in our
profession. And we can begin this work on department graduate and
program committees and at conferences and in professional publications.
Until we do, our commitment to collaborative writing is just another
fashion, just another hypocrisy. In all these actions, we can help
students to learn the ways in which they already *can* and *do* intervene
in the world though their composing and their reading of experiences.
And as our students learn their power, teachers will have to learn how
to let things happen. Writing is, after all, an event that makes other
events possible. There are things to do, despite our institutions, perhaps
because of them. There are incremental changes we can effect, and
there are ones that are jarring even to us.

Composition teachers must call more loudly for such teaching. We
have not, as a profession, dedicated ourselves to learning how to work
with students who have begun — and in some cases demanded — to take
control of the contexts that their writing creates. And, just as vital
to education, we need to resist perpetuating the contexts — and the
controls — that are imposed upon students and ourselves that serve
mainly to keep us all in line. In other words, teaching composition is
not teaching students lessons; it is teaching students — and ourselves —
to rewrite the lessons we have always already been taught. Louann
Reid and Jeff Golub argue that "Students need to learn how to control
their construction of knowledge." Joseph Harris and Jay Rosen discuss,
as does James Berlin, teaching writing as cultural critique. Miriam
Chaplin suggests that while students "may lack specific academic skills,
[they] have learned the lessons that a materialistic society has taught
them." Nancy Mack and James Zebroski, referring specifically to those
in the working class, write that students "need to actively write themselves into the language." And Marian Yee considers how students and
teachers can examine the ways in which they *are* already written into
language. Clearly, the participants in this collection are not simply
teaching people to read and write. In fact, they seem to suggest that
there is no such thing as simple reading and writing, nor the simple
teaching of them. Unfortunately, teaching people to write *well* often
means indoctrinating them, producing what Julia Lesage, specifically
writing about women's consciousness in our culture, calls "colonized
minds." For the two of us, reading Lesage's essay is a reminder that
our own teaching practices are deeply implicated in, among other

things, "a social process marked by male dominance and female submission" (420). Any generally *accepted* standards of excellence are,
likewise, marked. The question is, what will we *do* about it?

Perhaps as counter-educators we can teach students to challenge
the ways that formal education *fixes* what people say and do and think.
We can teach them to write and read as part of the complex web of
processes by which we shape our relations to other people, groups,
institutions, and ourselves. In other words, writing provides a way to
see how our knowledge fixes and damages social relations. And we
might start by asking the kinds of questions Patrick Shannon asks in
"The Struggle for Control of Literacy Lessons": What if students

> insisted that they be treated as active learners by everyone: teachers,
> administrators, parents, or employers? What if they demanded that
> all their learning environments be coherent, authentic, sensible, and
> purposeful? What if they expected that their language, experience,
> history, and culture be validated at school, at home, and at work?
> What if they believed and wrote and talked and acted as if we have
> free open language, free speech, free thought, and freedom to control
> our lives? What would it mean for our current social arrangement if
> middle-class, poor, and minority students understood the empower-
> ment of literacy by using it critically and independently...? (632)

Shannon's questions can be read as a proposal for specific kinds of
resistance that we suggest are both positive and radically unsettling to
social institutions. Specifically, these questions are about students—
people—taking literally the kinds of rights and freedoms that people in
positions of political/social/economic power *profess* to guarantee. In
response to Louann Reid's question—"how does one get the power to
speak?"—we ask, how has the power that people *do* have to speak
been lost or taken away? How have people managed so successfully
to censor their own speech? And what evidence of student resistance
to being silenced must composition teachers learn how to see and to
understand and to support? For students and teachers of composition,
the events that constitute writing also constitute, as Hélène Cixous
puts it, "precisely the *very possibility of change*, the space that can
serve as a springboard for subversive thought, precursory movement of
a transformation of social and cultural structures" (qtd. in Stimpson 11).

But we need to do a lot *more* than write a book in which we take
these issues up. We need to use *our* powers to speak—loudly and in as
many contexts as possible. We need to acknowledged and celebrate
the very significant work and actions that students do to resist merely
being "trained" in ways to accommodate and maintain the dominant
culture. Composition teachers can resist institutional pressure to
normalize and/or standardize discourse by encouraging students to

attend to differences in the ways that people use language, by supporting students' efforts to move back and forth (one meaning of interpretation) between dialects and styles. Composition teachers need to draw upon our strengths as readers of diverse, strange, sometimes elusive texts so that we can learn *from* our students' diversity. We need to listen to those most typically denied the legitimacy of their speech and their writing and their work.

Composition is a social arena — a field of social interactions and a result of social relations. The same must be said for compositions. And, we would argue, *Composition and Resistance* is a social event held in resistance to antisocial events taking place in higher education and in society. Movements such as English Only and U.S. English represent various people's efforts, not simply to argue for a normative form of English but for the legislation and litigation of restrictions on how people may and may not speak and write. Cultural literacy programs often serve to systematically exclude and/or deny the legitimacy of the real ways in which people use, shape, and are shaped by language. Even more sinister are the efforts by organizations such as The National Association of Scholars to deny both the political realities of and basic inequities in higher education and, for that matter, the world. The N.A.S. published a statement on the issue of bias in the curriculum, which included the remark, "Efforts purportedly made to introduce 'other points of view' and 'pluralism' often seem in fact designed to restrict attention to a narrow set of issues tendentiously defined. An examination of many women's studies and minority studies courses and programs discloses little study of other cultures and much excoriation of our society for its *alleged oppression of women, blacks, and others*" ("Is the Curriculum Biased?" Advertisement A23, our emphasis). What the N.A.S. evidently fears is higher education's loss of "objectivity," which "is in general not enhanced but subverted by the idea that people of different sexes, races, or ethnic backgrounds necessarily see things differently." But if people are *seen* differently, they — we — are bound to *see* differently. If this view means that we have "subverted" objectivity, let us be still more subversive.

In *Tenured Radicals: How Politics Has Corrupted Our Higher Education*, Roger Kimball argues that "Proponents of deconstruction, feminist studies, and other politically motivated challenges to the traitional tenets of humanistic study have by now become the dominant voice in the humanities departments of many of our best colleges and universities. And while there are differences and even struggles among these various groups, when seen from the perspective of the tradition that they are seeking to subvert — the tradition of high culture embodied in the classics of Western art and thought — they exhibit a remarkable unity of purpose. Their object is nothing less than the destruction of the values, methods, and goals of traditional humanistic study" (xi). Even if we could ignore the conservative elitism of Kimball's argument (we can't), we keep wondering why, if teachers who are sensitive to the political realities of American culture and education now dominate the educational scene, we don't see more change. Why are our schools and colleges still in such dire need of democratic reform? Why are teachers still teaching students to read and write in the restricted forms and for the restrictive purposes of traditional—and, yes, even the sometimes fashionable—academic writing? Why aren't more teachers calling for a greater openness to the possibilities created in the event(s) of student reading and writing? Surely, the theorists that Kimball talks about by name—some of whom have done work that we continue to learn from (Elaine Showalter and Houston Baker)—have targeted more than the "best colleges and universities"—whichever these are—to influence. If Kimball is correct about the dominance of subversive voices (an irony that betrays the academicization of cultural critique), we all ought to be seeing dramatic change where we teach.

Later in *Tenured Radicals*, Kimball argues that "the assault on the canon is not simply a matter of debasing the curriculum—of replacing Plato with Navaho folktales or Shakespeare with Jacqueline Susann. It also shows itself in the aggressively opaque jargons favored by many contemporary academics as well as in the widespread insinuation of patently political criteria into teaching" (2). If the canon and traditional humanistic knowledge and teaching are regarded as "transparent" in both their terminology and in their basic human goodness, perhaps the curriculum *ought* to be "debased," literally, shaken and contaminated. This may be the only chance we have of opening the classroom up to the teaching of Plato *and* Navaho folktales, Shakespeare *and* Jacqueline Susann, rap *as well as* papers of/on literary criticism, or better, critical papers infused with the power of rap—the power to speak for change by speaking in a new way and in and for a new place—by self-consciously calling for participation and action.

Composition and Resistance is an investigation of resistances and an act of resistance. Reading this book over and over, the two of us keep asking ourselves, how should we live with *settling* for what we *can* do when so much needs to be done? This book doesn't tell us how. But, to an extent, it shows us what to do. It offers the voices of English teachers who, while they clearly *don't* represent or speak for or with a dominant, unified voice, *do* talk and listen and write to learn how to make their teaching more meaningful in the context of social life. And after listening to the participants, we, Mark and Michael, propose that educators teach composition and literature in order to encourage *class actions*, resistances in our classrooms, profession, and private lives that any of us will make against those who use money, access to information, administrative rank, traditional privilege (male, white, heterosexual), to control other people, to deny them freedom and safety and equality and their voice, or to distract them/us from noticing the dangers of these conditions. This action demands that composition teachers *resist* teaching writing as something *for* a classroom. Writing shapes and is shaped by classroom experience, but the classroom must be a site of, not the sole reason for, the struggle that compositions invoke. We are suggesting that educators bear in mind, as Chantal Mouffe reminds us, that "people struggle for equality not because of some ontological postulate but because they have been constructed as subjects in a democratic tradition that puts those values at the center of social life" (95). Composition teachers must work with students to examine and intervene in the "constructions" that produce people as subjects and by which people subject other people to inequitable, abusive, intolerable conditions. Students can learn to trace particular and fundamental definitions of people and ideas as they are articulated in their compositions. Writing is the set of events in which notions such as these are redefined and are played out in their complex relations. Writing is one site, maybe the *one* site, where we are most powerful, most prepared for resistance, most ready *to begin* to act.

Works Cited

"Is the Curriculum Biased? A Statement by the National Association of Scholars." Advertisement. *Chronicle of Higher Education.* 8 Nov. 1989. A3.

Kimball, Roger. *Tenured Radicals: How Politics Has Corrupted Our Higher Education.* New York: Harper & Row, 1990.

Lesage, Julia. "Women's Rage." *Marxism and the Interpretation of Culture.* Eds. Cary Nelson and Lawrence Grossberg. Urbana: U of Illinois P, 1988, 491–28.

Mouffe, Chantal. "Hegemony and New Political Subjects: Toward a New Concept of Democracy." Trans. Stanley Gray. *Marxism and the Interpretation of Culture.* Eds. Cary Nelson and Lawrence Grossberg. Urbana: U of Illinois P, 1988. 89–104.

Shannon, Patrick. "The Struggle for Control of Literacy Lessons." *Language Arts* 66.6 (1989): 625–34.

Stallybrass, Peter, and Allon White. *The Politics and Poetics of Transgression.* Ithaca: Cornell UP, 1986.

Stimpson, Catharine R. "Gertrude Stein and the Transposition of Gender." *The Poetics of Gender.* Ed. Nancy K. Miller. New York: Columbia UP, 1986. 1–18.

Contributors

James A. Berlin Formerly an elementary school teacher in Detroit and Flint, Michigan, a composition teacher at Wichita State University, and a composition teacher and Director of Freshman English at the University of Cincinnati, I am now teaching in the English department at Purdue University. I have published two histories of writing instruction in U.S. colleges, both of which have been conspicuous by absence in the bibliographies of MLA-sponsored publications on the future of English Studies, despite the fact that the volume on the twentieth century was an honorable mention for the Mina Shaughnessy Prize. I am now studying the relations between cultural studies and English studies, past, present, and future.

Miriam T. Chaplin I am an Associate Professor of Education at Rutgers University, Camden. I received my undergraduate degree at St. Joseph's University, masters at Temple University, and doctoral degree from Rutgers University, New Brunswick. I have taught at all levels of education, and I consider this one of the advantages of my career. This broad perspective allows me to view the teaching/learning process from the very early years through graduate school. As a practitioner, I believe this is extremely important. Most recently, I have directed my attention to an understanding of literacy that is different from the traditional view. My article in this book speaks to that interest.

Judith Fetterley I am a Professor of English and Women's Studies at the University at Albany/State University of New York. As Director of Graduate Studies for the Department of English since 1987, I have worked with colleagues to develop a new doctoral program in "Writing, Teaching, and Criticism." I have written *The Resisting Reader: A Feminist Approach to American Fiction* and *Provisions: A Reader from Nineteenth-Century American Women*, as well as various articles on nineteenth- and twentieth-century American writers. With Joanne Dobson and Elaine Showalter, I initiated the American Women Writers series, published by Rutgers University Press, which reprints works by nineteenth- and early twentieth-century American women writers. For this series, I edited a volume of the short fiction of Alice Cary. With Marjorie Pryse I have co-authored the *Norton Anthology of American Women Regionalist Writers, 1850–1920* (forthcoming, December 1991); and together we are working on a full-length critical study of the writers included in this anthology.

Jeff Golub I am a teacher of English, Speech Communication, and Pre-College Writing classes at Shorecrest High School in Seattle, Washington. I also work extensively with the National Council of Teachers of English, having served as Representative-at-Large on the NCTE Executive Committee and edited two books for the Council, one on critical thinking and the other on collaborative learning. I am especially interested in the instructional opportunities available through telecommunications. By having my students exchange notes and other correspondence electronically with other classrooms around the country and around the world, I am able to provide them with real audiences and real purposes for their communications efforts.

Joseph Harris I am an assistant professor of English at the University of Pittsburgh, where I teach undergraduate courses in writing, film, and literature, and graduate seminars in the teaching of composition and English. My article on "The Idea of Community in the Study of Writing" (CCC, February 1989) won the 1990 Braddock Award, and I am currently at work on a study of the recent constructing of "composition" as an academic discipline.

C. Mark Hurlbert and Michael Blitz We, Mark and Michael, have been writing and arguing since 1985. Our articles include: "To: You, From: Michael Blitz and C. Mark Hurlbert, Re: Literacy Demands and Institutional Autobiography," "Toward an Poetics in the Age of Intersubjectivity," "Cults of Culture," and "The Institution('s) Lives!" We are husbands to Terry and Karen and fathers to Roland, Daina, and a baby to be named later.

C. H. Knoblauch I'm an Associate Professor of English, and currently the director of graduate studies, at the University at Albany, SUNY. I teach undergraduate introductions to literature and literary theory, along with beginning and advanced writing courses and graduate seminars in rhetorical theory, literacy studies, and pedagogy. As chair of a University committee aiming to redesign our writing program and our general education curriculum, I have some hope of attracting the stern gaze of the National Association of Scholars, whose irritation will assure me, as it is assuring others, that I'm doing something worthwhile.

Nancy Mack I have taught middle school students, prison inmates, and college students. I am currently an Assistant Professor in the English department at Wright State University. I teach undergraduate courses in composition and graduate courses in classroom practices for teachers. I spend a great deal of time with teachers in whole language support groups, school district inservices, and state professional organizations. Current projects include: an annual summer institute, Writing and Its Teaching, and forthcoming essays in *Social Issues in the English Classroom, Supporting Whole Language* (Heinemann), and *PRE/ TEXT: A Journal of Rhetorical Theory.* I am married and have two children ages six and twelve.

Stephen M. North I am an associate professor of English at SUNY Albany, where I also serve as Director of the English Department's Writing Program. I have published articles in a number of professional journals, and authored one book, *The Making of Knowledge in Composition* (Boynton/Cook). My professional concerns seem to revolve around the forms and sources of authority. These days, I am especially interested in notions of "personal voice" and common sense, with an abiding interest in the relationship between ideas like these and what it means to be a teacher.

Louann Reid   Next to learning, there is nothing more important than teaching; frequently, the two cannot be separated. Currently I learn from my high school students in courses ranging from reading to literature to composition and from coaching the forensics team. I teach Methods of Secondary English at the University of Denver on Saturdays and expect to receive a Ph.D. in English Education from New York University in 1991. Involvement in professional organizations, such as NCTE and the Colorado Language Arts Society, and collaboration with colleagues have helped shape my ideas about interaction, reflection, and composition.

Cecilia Rodríguez Milanés   I taught ESOL to elementary school children and then English to African American and Latino high school students in Miami before attending the State University of New York at Albany where I earned a Doctor of Arts in Composition. While at SUNYA I taught introductory literature and writing courses, worked in the Writing Center, and served as the writing consultant to the Women's Studies Department. I have recently accepted a position at Indiana University of Pennsylvania where I hope to continue to write about issues of ethnicity, gender, and class—though not necessarily in that order.

Jay Rosen   I am an assistant professor of journalism and mass communications at New York University, where I am also an associate at the Center for War, Peace, and the News Media. My writings have appeared in the *Los Angeles Times, Harpers, The Progressive, Tikkun, Newsday*, and other journals. In 1990–91, I was a Research Fellow at the Gannett Center for Media Studies at Columbia University.

Donna Singleton   In keeping with my chapter, I prefer to identify myself as a teacher/learner, both within the classroom and without. I enjoy helping others teach themselves what they want and need to learn. Currently I am learning about the teaching of writing from students in my freshman classes and about the teaching of high school English from the student teachers I supervise. I am especially interested in finding better ways for teachers to respond to student writing. Besides formal "schooling" in German, English, and composition, I continue to learn informally about parenting from my two terrific daughters, about writing from friends and rejection slips, and about living from everyone I meet.

James Sledd   I have taught in altogether too many places, and in each of which I have talked and written too much. I am now in retirement at Clown's Delight, Sur Pedernales.

Kurt Spellmeyer   For the last six years I have been the Director of the Writing Program at Rutgers University in New Brunswick. I have published articles on composition in *College English*, and my book, *Common Ground: Difference, Understanding, and the Teaching of Composition*, is forthcoming from Prentice Hall in 1991.

J. Elspeth Stuckey   I am the director of the South Carolina Cross-Age Tutorial Program affiliated with Clemson University and South Carolina State.

Marian Yee I am a graduate student in English at Rutgers University.

James Thomas Zebroski I work at Syracuse University teaching undergraduate and graduate courses in writing and rhetoric. I received my three degress from The Ohio State University, having taught in the public schools and at colleges in Ohio, Texas, and Pennsylvania. I am a writer and teacher who sees theory as a way to generate and problematize teaching and curricular practices. My research on the psychosocial theory of Lev Vygotsky and composition practices complements my work on M. M. Bakhtin. Of current importance for me is making sense of the ways my working-class, ethnic heritage has composed me and my writing.